Steerage and Steel

Steerage and Steel

True Stories of Titanic's Immigrants and Crew

By Alina Rush

Unbound Press

Steerage and Steel: True Stories of Titanic's Immigrants and Crew

Fault Lines: Book 1

Alina Rush

ISBN Paperback 978-1-971207-11-7

ISBN Hardcover 978-1-971207-12-4

The Fault Lines Series

The Fault Lines series examines moments when progress, confidence, and modern systems collide—and fail. These books focus not on spectacle or hindsight, but on the underlying fractures that disasters expose: labor rendered invisible, class shaping survival, technology trusted beyond its limits, and institutions slow to confront their own assumptions.

Beginning with the Titanic trilogy and extending to crises such as the economic disparities of the Great Depression, the series traces how economic, social, and technological fault lines run beneath seemingly stable worlds. Each volume grounds its narrative in verifiable history while centering the experiences of ordinary people caught inside extraordinary events—workers, immigrants, families, and communities whose lives bore the actual cost of collapse.

Fault Lines is not a history of accidents. It is a study of systems under stress, of warnings ignored, and of the human consequences that follow when risk is unevenly distributed. These are stories about how societies break—and what those breaks reveal long after the headlines fade.

Contents

Dedication

To those who find light in darkness, who choose courage over comfort, and whose hope illuminates the path forward.

"Forever in our hearts."

Introduction

The first thing most people remember about Titanic is what happened on the top decks: the band, the lifeboats, the grand staircase, the famous names. That version of the story is not wrong—but it is incomplete in the way that myths are incomplete. It is the Titanic remembered from above.

This book begins below.

Steerage was not just "third class"—it was an ecosystem of families, single travelers, and communities in motion. Down below, families lay shoulder to shoulder in narrow bunks, surrounded by trunks, bundled bedding, and the weight of everything they could not afford to bring. Languages overlapped in the corridors—Irish, Swedish, Finnish, Italian, Arabic, English—each voice carrying the same hope in different words: a new start.

The crew was not a single category either; it was a hierarchy of labor, authority, and exhaustion. In the workspaces beyond the passenger decks, men shoveled coal for furnace heat, hauled ash, oiled machinery, and measured their shifts not by sunlight but by whistles and schedules. Wireless operators, stewards, and lookouts kept the ship functioning with their invisible labor. The ship's luxury depended on them. Its speed depended on their bodies. Its order depended on their obedience.

They are rarely the center of Titanic's story. They should be.

Titanic was not only a maritime disaster. It was a floating map of the early twentieth century—of wealth and poverty, of empire and industry, of migration and ambition, of rules designed to separate people and keep them in their place. Class was built into the ship's architecture. It shaped where you slept, what you ate, which corridors you could walk through, which doors you could open, which information reached you first, and what chances you had when everything went wrong.

That is why the lower decks matter. Not because they provide a grittier backdrop for the same famous tale, but because they reveal Titanic as it truly was: a society under steam.

This book follows two groups whose experiences are often treated as footnotes—immigrants and crew—not because their stories are marginal, but because they are central to what Titanic meant. The immigrants carried the future in battered luggage: the promise of jobs, family reunions, escape from hardship, and a chance at dignity on the far side of the Atlantic. The crew carried the ship itself: stokers and trimmers feeding the boilers, greasers keeping engines alive, stewards running corridors, sailors tending lines, and workers whose names never became legend because their work was always unseen.

Their worlds overlapped more than the usual retellings admit. Both groups lived inside the unseen machinery of modern life: schedules, compartments, rules, gatekeeping, and the belief—explicit and enforced—that some lives were meant to have more access than others.

When the collision came, those differences did not vanish. They sharpened.

Most narratives of the sinking focus on the ship's command and its officers' decisions. Titanic was not commanded into tragedy by a single decision or failure. It was built to carry inequality across an ocean, and when crisis struck, inequality became destiny for many.

This book stays close to the record: passenger lists, crew rosters, contemporary newspaper reporting, official investigations, letters, memoirs, and the scattered fragments families saved because they could not bear to lose everything. Where the record is uncertain, it will be treated as uncertain. Where testimony conflicts, the conflict will be shown. If a detail survives only as legend, it will be labeled as such, not smuggled in as fact.

But this is not a story made only of documents. It is a story made of people.

It is a mother counting children in a chaotic corridor with instructions she cannot fully understand. It is a father calculating, in a few seconds, whether to stay with his family or race upward to find help. It is a young man traveling alone or a crewman who knows the ship by heart and still cannot control what water will do once it has found a way in.

It is the quiet, brutal truth that "women and children first" meant something different depending on which deck you lived on and which doors were between you and the boats.

It is also the aftermath—because for immigrants and crew, the story does not end when the Carpathia arrives. Survival was not a clean ending. It meant poverty, injuries, grief, and the strange burden of being alive when others were not. For families who lost everyone, the aftermath was paperwork and silence: bodies unidentified, stories flattened into a line on a list. For the crew, it was often blame without recognition—asked to answer for a catastrophe that the world insisted must have been someone's fault.

And yet, amid all that, there is what makes these histories worth telling: resilience. The stubborn insistence that the class of ticket does not measure a life it carried. The truth is that some of the most consequential stories in history belong to people who never had a platform, never wrote a memoir, and never saw their names on a plaque.

If you came to this book looking for the Titanic you already know—the famous passengers, the grand symbols—you will still find the ship's outlines here, because that Titanic is the setting no one can ignore. But the center of gravity shifts. The emphasis turns to the spaces most retellings rush past: the narrow stairwells, gates, boiler rooms, and the deck edges where instruction turned into panic and panic turned into fate.

This is Titanic as experienced by the people who made it move, and the people who trusted it with everything they owned.

This is the story carried in steerage and forged in steel.

Part I — The Two Titanics

Chapter 1 — A Society Under Steam

"Pride goeth before destruction, and a haughty spirit before a fall."

—Book of Proverbs, 16:18

TITANIC DID NOT SIMPLY carry people across the Atlantic. It arranged them.

Before a single lifeboat was swung out, before a single iceberg warning was logged, the ship had already made its most consequential decision: it turned social class into architecture. The divisions that shaped daily life on land — money, language, status, labor — were built into the steel corridors, deck access, dining rooms, and doors.

Francis Godolphin Osbourne Stuart, Public domain, via Wikimedia Commons

If you traveled first class, the ship was a statement. If you traveled in steerage, it was a system. If you worked the voyage, it was a machine you fed with hours, sweat, and compliance.

The Two Titanics

There were, in practice, at least two Titanics moving through the same water.

The public Titanic was the one photographed, described, and sold to the world. A ship of gleaming public rooms, wide promenades, and polished ritual. It was built to reassure. The White Star Line's promise was not only speed; it was stability. The ship was marketed as modern, safe, and comfortable, a floating hotel that made the Atlantic feel smaller and less frightening.

But the hidden Titanic was the one that made the public Titanic possible. It was a ship of narrow passageways, shared spaces, strict rules, and controlled movement. It was a ship where work and migration were not themes but realities. The people there did not talk about the ship as a marvel. They talked about what it cost, what it meant, and what it might change.

For many immigrant families, Titanic was a single pivot point: the moment between a life they were leaving and one they hoped would be better. They carried addresses on paper, names of relatives to find, the promise of jobs, and the belief that America could be remade through endurance.

For crew members, Titanic represented something different: a contract, a wage, a hierarchy. For the crew, the Atlantic was not an ocean to cross; it was a workplace to endure.

These realities existed on the same ship, yet they did not receive the same protections, information, or opportunities. That is not moral commentary. It is a structural description. And structure matters.

What "Steerage" Really Meant

"Third class" sounds tidy. "Steerage" sounds like something older, rougher, and less dignified—and the language matters because it reveals what was expected.

Steerage passengers came from different nations, religions, trades, family structures, and social worlds. Some were traveling alone, aiming to earn money and send it home. Others were families in motion, heading toward relatives already settled. Some were skilled workers. Some were agricultural laborers. Some were fleeing political pressures, religious constraints, or local economies that had failed them.

What they shared was not identity. It was placement.

Steerage accommodations were designed for volume, sanitation, and control, not for comfort or leisure. Most passengers slept in shared cabins or dormitory-style spaces, often with stacked berths. Privacy was minimal. Noise and smells carried. The ship was engineered to reduce disease risk compared with older steerage travel, but it was still a crowded living environment.

Titanic The Artifact Exhibition Boston Third Class Cabin 2025

Third-class passengers had access to a male-only smoking room, two dining rooms (divided by a bulkhead), and a general room that served as both a lounge and a nursery, which became a recreational area each evening.

Cabins in third class included bunk beds for 4 to 6 people, a sink, and a small wardrobe. Private toilets in the ship's cabins were unheard of and not even available in second class. Large, well-maintained public toilets, similar to those we see today in public spaces and restaurants, were provided, along with showers and baths.

The third-class experience also depended on who one traveled with. Entire clusters of passengers from the same region or language group were sometimes found aboard, forming temporary communities—translating rules, sharing information, and helping one another navigate shipboard life.

It is essential to say this plainly: steerage life was not uniformly miserable. Many immigrants were accustomed to hardship and saw the ship's conditions as a tolerable price for a new start. But steerage life was always constrained, and constraints become critical in an emergency.

Because when the ship struck the iceberg, steerage passengers did not begin the night with equal access to the outside decks. They began it with questions: What happened? Where do we go? Which corridor leads upward? Which door is for us? Who will translate? Will we be permitted through?

A ship built to manage people smoothly in ordinary times can become a trap when time becomes extraordinary.

The Crew: Not One Group, But a Ladder of Labor

Titanic's crew is often spoken of as if it were a single class of men in uniform. However, on a large passenger liner, crew work was divided into departments with distinct authorities, risks, and levels of visibility. Passengers constantly saw some crew members: stewards, dining-room staff, officers, and perhaps a few deckhands. Others worked out of sight: engine-room teams, firemen, trimmers, greasers—men whose labor powered the ship but rarely entered the public imagination.

There was a ladder within the labor force itself. Officers held authority and status. Many other crew members were disposable, as industrial labor often is: replaceable bodies assigned to exhausting work.

Some crew roles were physically punishing even in regular operation. Boiler-room and engine-room work involved heat, coal dust, noise, and constant motion. It was not heroic in the romantic sense. It was relentless. It was measured in shifts and endurance.

This matters for the same reason as steerage issues of structure: in a disaster, you do not suddenly become equal. You move according to the job you were hired to do and the space you were assigned to inhabit.

A crewman assigned below decks could not simply abandon his post without consequences—formal, cultural, and practical. In a crisis, some men stayed because they were ordered to. Some stayed because they believed it was the right thing. Some stayed because leaving would have been physically difficult or impossible. The result is the same: the ship's "hidden" workforce often had less opportunity to reach safety than the people they served.

The Gatekeeping Ship

Ships of this era were designed with controlled access: class-segregated stairways, corridors that funneled people toward specific spaces, and doors that directed traffic. Some of these boundaries were cultural—unspoken rules reinforced by staff. Others were literal—gates, partitions, posted areas, and staffed doors.

In ordinary times, such systems reduce chaos. They keep meals running. They prevent crowding. They preserve the illusion that different social worlds can coexist without friction.

In a crisis, those same systems can delay information, slow evacuation, and turn uncertainty into panic. For immigrants unfamiliar with the ship's layout—especially those navigating language barriers—delay is not a minor inconvenience. Delay is survival math.

This is one of the core truths of Titanic: class shaped time. Time to learn what happened. Time to understand the orders. Time to reach the deck and find a boat. The time to decide.

When people argue about whether steerage was "held back," the debate often devolves into a simplistic accusation. The reality is that systems designed for control in normal operation perform poorly under stress. People within those systems make choices—some generous, some indifferent, some fearful, some cruel. The architecture itself quietly takes sides.

To tell the story correctly, we have to understand the ship before the collision: not as a legend, but as a functioning society. A ship that offered luxury to some, passage to others, and employment to many—then demanded that all of them respond to catastrophe from very different starting positions.

Chapter 2 — All Aboard

"The horizon leans forward, offering you space to place new steps of change."

– Maya Angelou

IN THE SPRING OF 1909, on the gray edge of Belfast Lough, men in flat caps and heavy boots walked beneath a wall of steel. Above them, the ribs of a new ship—Yard Number 401—rose higher than any building in the city. She was not yet called Titanic. She was an idea first: an answer to rival shipping lines, a promise of crossing the sea in unmatched comfort and safety.

By the time her hull slid down the greased ways on May 31, 1911, cheered by a crowd of more than 100,000, Titanic was already famous, already a symbol of what modern steel and steam could achieve.

The White Star Promise

At the dawn of the 20th century, as empires traded people and goods across the North Atlantic, competition among shipping companies intensified. Rival lines boasted of speed and elegance, famous passengers, and record-breaking passages, and the White Star Line responded with a different promise: not just the fastest crossing, but the most comfortable and prestigious way to reach America.

From this promise came a trio of great liners, the Olympic-class ships—Olympic, Titanic, and a planned third sister, later named Britannic—intended to dominate the Atlantic in 1911, 1912, and 1913.

In Belfast, Ireland, the Harland & Wolff shipyard reshaped itself to meet that ambition. New gantries rose above the water, taller than any building in the city, and beneath them thousands of men filed in each morning, lunch tins in hand, to work on a vessel called Yard Number 401. On March 31, 1909, the first keel plates were laid on the slipway, and the ship's skeleton began to climb into the gray Belfast sky, each steel rib another step toward what many in the press were already calling a "floating palace."

For more than two years, the work did not stop. Riveters hammered red-hot metal into place; cranes swung great sections of the hull into position; nearby sheds turned out fittings for cabins that would rival grand hotels on land. White Star's goal was clear: a ship large enough to carry wealthy travelers in luxury and, at the same time, to move thousands of emigrants in third-class and hundreds of crew members across the ocean in a steady, profitable stream. Speed mattered, but prestige mattered more.

On May 31, 1911, to the sound of whistles and cheers from a crowd reported to be in the tens of thousands, the great steel form slid down her greased ways into the water of Belfast Lough. She was officially named Titanic, the second of the Olympic-class sisters, and in that moment, she became, in sheer size, the largest moving man-made object in the world.[1]

Her launch was only the beginning. Inside her empty hull, an army of carpenters, electricians, plumbers, and decorators worked for months, transforming bare steel into paneled saloons, dining rooms, boiler rooms, galleys, and cramped crew quarters. Deep inside the ship, giant boilers and engines were installed to drive her across the Atlantic; above, craftsmen laid carpets and fitted marble, glass, and woodwork for first-class spaces, while third-class accommodations, though simple, were still better than many emigrants' housing on land.

Titanic was designed to carry about 2,435 passengers and around 900 crew, a small floating city divided by class and function yet sharing the same steel hull and the same cold ocean. Her designers built in fifteen watertight bulkheads and doors that could be closed from the bridge, a system widely praised at the time and often cited as a reason she was described in newspapers and advertisements as practically "unsinkable."

On March 31, 1912, Titanic's construction was declared complete, and preparations began to move her from a ship under construction to one in service. On April 2, she went to sea for her trials—short tests of speed, handling, and safety systems—after which officials signed the documents certifying her seaworthiness. From there, she steamed to Southampton, England, her designated home port for the transatlantic run.

Titanic arrived at Southampton's White Star Dock, Berth 44, in the early hours of April 4, 1912, docking stern-first to prepare for its maiden voyage.[2] The ship's three towering funnels (a fourth stood above as a dummy for ventilation and appearance) and her long, clean decks gave an impression of power and confidence that matched the age that had built her.

Coal wagons arrived and dumped tons of fuel into her bunkers; cranes swung cargo, mailbags, and baggage aboard; provisions—meat, flour, vegetables, wine, and simple staples for third-class—were loaded to feed passengers and crew for a week at sea.

Crew members reported to the shipping office, signed their names, and found their assigned quarters and duties, from officers on the bridge to firemen in the boiler rooms and stewards assigned to first-, second-, or third-class passengers.

Titanic in Southampton, England, Public Domain

The Docks

Long before Titanic met ice, it met people—standing in lines, clutching papers, watching smoke drift from funnels, trying to look steady while their lives shifted behind their eyes.

For first-class passengers, the dock could feel like a stage: porters, trunks, and goodbyes framed as ritual. For steerage passengers, it was something else: a sorting gate. A place where you were measured, tagged, and directed into the right corridor.

And for the crew, it was the beginning of work— another ship, another contract, another set of rules that would follow them across the Atlantic.

A Ship That Promised the Future

Titanic belonged to a new era of ocean travel, and it was sold as proof that the future had arrived. People didn't just buy a ticket; they bought assurance—about comfort, safety, and modern engineering, about the idea that you could cross an ocean without fear.

That promise mattered most to the people who had the least margin for error.

An immigrant family's passage was rarely a casual purchase. A Third Class ticket on the Titanic cost roughly $30-40 in 1912, about $500 to $900 today. By comparison, First Class tickets were around $4,500 in equivalent value. It could represent years of saving, borrowed money, or a relative's sacrifice. It could represent a plan built on thin threads: an address written down, a promised job, a cousin waiting at a station, a rumor that work was plentiful in a city you had never seen. If the crossing failed, you didn't simply miss a vacation. You lost the bridge between your past and your future.

For these travelers, the dock held more than luggage. It held stakes.

The Sorting Begins

Titanic's society didn't begin at sea. It began before embarkation, in the procedures that governed who boarded, how they were documented, and where they were directed once they stepped onto the ship.

Steerage passengers moved through a process designed for control and compliance. They were handled in groups: checked, recorded, and managed by staff whose job was to keep the stream of bodies moving, keep the paperwork clean, and keep the classes separate.

The lines were physical, yet they also carried something invisible: status. It was always present in how people were addressed, where they were told to wait, how much space they were allowed to take up on the dock, and how quickly they were encouraged to disappear into the ship. For many immigrants, the first shock of the crossing wasn't the ocean. It was the system.

Tickets, Names, and the Fragility of Identity

To travel in steerage was to learn how easily a clerk's pen could alter your identity.

Names were written down, copied, and recopied. Spellings shifted. Languages collided with forms not built for them. A person could become a slightly different person before ever reaching the ship. A name with a diacritic became plain. A long surname was shortened. A first name was changed into something the clerk could write quickly.

For some, these changes were minor. For others, they became permanent. Titanic's paperwork became part of the story.

Luggage: What People Carried When They Carried Everything

Steerage luggage was rarely decorative. It was often practical to the point of austerity: clothing, tools, family documents, and a few objects that survived the choice of what to leave behind.

Trunks were more than containers. A skilled laborer might carry tools because the tools were his future wages. A mother might carry extra blankets because the ship's bedding wasn't trusted, or because a child's comfort mattered more than the weight. Families brought food items when they could, not because the ship promised nothing, but because past crossings had taught them not to rely on promises. If first class demonstrated wealth, steerage revealed strategy.

The luggage would later tell its own story when trunks and Suitcases were hauled up from the seabed years later, their contents eerily intact—work clothes folded and pressed, papers carefully tucked away, the modest instruments of lives that had been planned but never lived.

The Clusters: How Immigrants Found One Another

In third class, people rarely traveled alone. They moved in clusters—cousins alongside cousins, neighbors from the same village, families linked by language and the quiet mathematics of chain migration. Even strangers sought the comfort of recognition. In the din of a crowded ship, you listened for your own language. You searched for faces that carried the contours of home. You gravitated toward those who seemed to grasp the rules more quickly, hoping their certainty might become your own.

On the docks, these clusters formed and dissolved, then formed again. They translated unfamiliar words, kept watch for swindlers, and counted one another's bags, creating small, fragile communities long before the ship ever left the pier. They held children while papers were examined. They stood together because standing alone felt like risk.

The Crew: Men Who Boarded to Work, Not to Arrive

While immigrant families were focused on what awaited them in America, crew members approached Titanic as a workplace. Their relationship to the ship was contractual, hierarchical, and often harsh.

A crewman signing on did not imagine New York as a destination in the same way passengers did. For many, New York was a turnaround point, a port where the ship would be serviced and the next cycle of labor would begin. Routes, rosters shaped their lives, and the realities of sea work: the vessel was home, and home was a place where rules were enforced by rank.

The crew was also sorted by department, job, and authority. A steward's world differed from a fireman's, and a sailor's from a trimmer's. Titanic's crew were divided into three principal departments: the deck, with 66 crew, engine, with 325, and victualling, with 494. The vast majority of the crew were thus not seamen but were either engineers, firemen, or stokers, responsible for looking after the engines, or stewards and galley staff, responsible for the passengers. Of these, over 97% were male; just 23 of the crew were female, mainly stewardesses.

The rest represented a variety of professions—bakers, chefs, butchers, fishmongers, dishwashers, stewards, gymnasium instructors, laundrymen, waiters, bed-makers, cleaners, and even a printer, who produced a daily newspaper for passengers called the Atlantic Daily Bulletin with the latest news received by the ship's wireless operators.

The crew boarded with less luggage and fewer illusions. Many had seen ships before. Titanic was new, yes—but a ship is still a ship, and work at sea remains work at sea.

The Moment of Boarding

There is a moment, as you step from the dock onto the gangway, when the world behind you becomes less reachable. For first class, it can feel like departure; for steerage, like surrender. The ship absorbs you into its corridors and rules—the air changes. The vessel's scale makes you feel small.

For immigrant families, boarding Titanic could be the first time they had ever stood on a ship of such size. It could also be the first time they had ever been processed—inspected, recorded, and managed—in such a formal way. The crossing was not just a journey across water; it was a journey into a system.

On that dock, all of them—immigrants, crew, and passengers of every class—shared one belief, whether they admitted it or not: that the ship would do what ships were built to do.

It would carry them through.

Titanic leaving Southampton, April
Public domain, via Wikimedia Commons

[1] "Building the Titanic," Titanic Facts.

[2] "Titanic in Southampton," British Titanic Society.

Part II — The Voyage Begins

Chapter 3 — Underway

"Man cannot discover new oceans unless he has the courage to lose sight of the shore."

– André Gide

At 11:45 A.M. ON April 10, 1912, as lines were cast off and tugs eased her from the quay, Titanic's deep steam whistles sounded across the harbor.

The great liner moved slowly down Southampton Water, beginning her maiden voyage to New York—a journey meant to prove that this vast new ship, built for comfort and strength, could cross the Atlantic as smoothly and safely as her builders promised.

But leaving port didn't go as planned.

The maiden voyage began at noon, as scheduled. Within minutes of getting underway, Titanic demonstrated the unsettling physics of her own size. As she slid past the moored liners City of New York and Oceanic, the sheer displacement of her hull pulled the water out from beneath them, lifting both ships on a swelling surge before dropping them hard into the trough that followed.

The strain proved too much. New York's mooring lines snapped one by one, and the ship swung loose, stern first, drifting directly toward Titanic's flank. A tugboat, Vulcan, rushed in and took New York under tow as Captain Smith ordered Titanic's engines full astern. The great liner shuddered, slowed, and—by a margin measured in feet rather than yards—the two ships slid past one another, missing collision by scarcely four feet. The incident delayed Titanic's departure for about an hour, while the drifting New York was brought under control.

At around 1 p.m. she finally made it out to sea, and began her journey headed to New York.

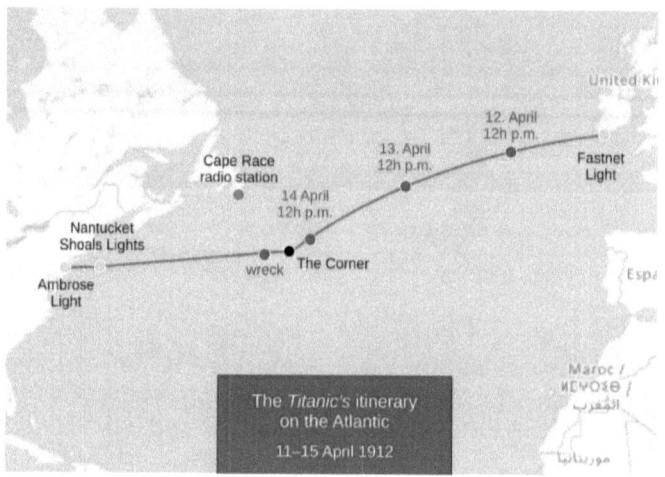

The Titanic's itinerary on the Atlantic

11–15 April 1912

The Lives on Board

In total, 920 passengers boarded Titanic at Southampton: 179 in First Class, 247 in Second Class, and 494 in Third Class. Additional passengers were taken aboard at Cherbourg and Queenstown.

While passenger lists reduce individuals to categories: age, sex, occupation, nationality, and class, they miss the humanity of the people behind the statistics, who carried the quiet courage of leaving everything familiar behind.

The Anderssons: A Family in Motion

Among the steerage passengers were the Anderssons—Scandinavian emigrants whose voyage was not a single leap but the final stage of a longer migration chain. Unlike the slightly melodramatic portrayal of impoverished yet inexplicably cheerful third-class passengers in James Cameron's *Titanic*, the real vessel's steerage accommodations were more expensive than those on most other liners, resulting in White Star Line's third-class clientele being predominantly upper working-class or lower middle-class.

Andersson Family before 1912

By 1912, patterns of migration from Sweden to North America were well established. People left rural areas and small towns to work in industry abroad or to follow relatives who had already settled. Entire family decisions could hinge on one job lead, one cousin's letter, or one employer willing to sponsor or recommend.

Anders Johan Andersson received such a letter. In 1912, he was 39 years old, a farmer in Kisa, Östergötland, Sweden, working land that provided his family with security and a way of life that met most of their needs. By local standards, they were quite well off, rooted in a place where they knew every field and neighbor. He and his wife, Alfrida, had built a busy household together, with five children—Ebba, Ellis, Ingeborg, Sigrid, and little Sigvard—filling the farmhouse with activity and motion.

But another world called to them from across the Atlantic. Letters arrived from Alfrida's sister, Anna Danborn, who had already gone ahead and described the vast spaces and opportunities in North America. The pull of family began to outweigh the comfort of familiar soil. The decision to leave was not made lightly; it meant selling what they could, saying goodbye to the farm at Kättestorp, and trusting that the promise of a better future justified the risk.

In the end, the bond between sisters—Anna waiting in Canada, Alfrida still in Sweden—tilted the balance.

Accompanying the family on their journey was Anna Nysten, 22, from Farsbo, just outside Kisa. Her sister, Elsa, had relocated to New Jersey about a decade earlier, and Anna was drawn by the promise of employment and more opportunities in America.

The journey began not with the sea but with the iron rails that cut across Sweden. Anders and Alfrida gathered their children and whatever belongings they could carry, then boarded a train from Kisa to Gothenburg, the first leg of a journey that would draw them from their rural life toward Europe's great ports.[1]

In Gothenburg, they traded the steady sway of the train for a smaller ship that would take them across the North Sea to Hull on England's east coast. For the children, it was an exciting world of new sounds and smells—coal smoke, crowded decks, the restless motion of water beneath the hull.

Anna Nysten

At Hull, they spent the night, and the next day another train arrived, this time bound for Southampton, the busy port from which so many emigrants departed for the New World. There, for a few days, the Andersson family waited with their luggage, part of a tide of third-class passengers from many countries, all funneling toward the same destination.

They received word in Southampton that their passage had been canceled because of a coal strike. However, a transfer to a large White Star Line vessel was offered, and Anders, Alfrida, and Sophia made their final, fateful purchase: third-class tickets on a new ship whose name was already famous—Titanic. The tickets gave them a cabin in the ship's aft section, deep within the vessel, where families like theirs were quartered together, far from the grand saloons and promenades of first-class.

For the Andersson children, the sheer size of the vessel must have been overwhelming; for their parents, it was a mixture of anxiety and hope, a belief that this floating city would carry them safely to Anna's home in Winnipeg, Canada, where kinship and opportunity awaited on the far side of the ocean.

For a family traveling together, Titanic represented a concentrated gamble: if the crossing succeeded, the family arrived intact; if it failed, the loss was total. Large steerage families carried extra complexity from the start—children to manage, luggage to track, language to navigate, and the constant responsibility of keeping the group together in crowded spaces where separation could happen quickly.

On board, steerage families like the Anderssons were also more visible than single travelers. Children demanded space and attention, and parents had to learn the ship's ins and outs while protecting the family's rhythm: meals, rest, clothing, and small comforts that eased fear. In an unfamiliar environment, routine becomes essential.

The Syrian and Lebanese Passengers: Faith, Family, and Distance

Among the steerage passengers were travelers from the Eastern Mediterranean—often referred to in era records as "Syrians," reflecting the political geography and terminology of the time. Many were Christians from communities facing economic strain and social pressures, and they had already begun forming migration networks to North America.

In the opening years of the twentieth century, a steady stream of Arab migrants set out for the United States, driven by poverty, conscription, and political uncertainty under Ottoman rule. Many came from small villages in what is now Lebanon and Syria, carrying addresses scribbled on scraps of paper and the expectation that kin awaited them on the far shore.

They were not heading into the unknown so much as toward something already begun. Relatives had gone ahead, carving out footholds in places like Detroit and Cleveland, or in the coal towns of Pennsylvania, and their letters pulled others across the Atlantic, village by village, family by family. Families and neighbors followed one

another. Chain migration created corridors of movement—
specific villages connected to specific American cities
through letters, remittances, and sponsorship.

These passengers complicate a simplistic view of Titanic
steerage as predominantly Northern European. The lower
decks carried a wider world. Diverse foods, languages,
and customs, and the constant negotiation of identity in
spaces structured around English-language authority.

For many immigrants from the Middle East, the Atlantic
crossing was not merely long—it was disorienting. The
journey connected regions that had little direct contact. It
required trust in brokers, ticket agents, transit schedules,
and officials at multiple checkpoints. A single mistake
could derail everything.

For families, the risks multiplied: children needed care,
older relatives required support, and the whole group
depended on staying together through the machinery of
travel.

Tu'mah Family — Lebanese Passengers

Hinnah Tu'mah was born on April 10, 1885, in Tibnīn, a
hill town in southern Lebanon, when the region was still
part of the Ottoman Empire. She married young, around
age 15, to Darwīsh Tu'mah, an onion farmer five years her
senior. Together, they began raising a family in the same
countryside that had shaped their parents and
grandparents.

By the time she was in her twenties, she had two
children—Mariyam, born in 1902, and Jirjis Yūsuf, born in

1904—small hands at her skirts as she moved between home and fields.

Life in Tibnīn offered continuity but few opportunities. In 1905, like many men from the Levant seeking work abroad, Darwīsh left Lebanon and made his way to the United States, eventually settling in Silver Creek, Michigan. There, he worked on a farm, sending what he could back home and saving toward a single goal: buying his own land in nearby Dowagiac and bringing his wife and children to join him.

He purchased his own farm in 1911. More than a parcel of property, it was a promise that the family would not have to live apart.

For Hinnah, the call to leave came one year later. In February 1912, she gathered what little they could carry and began the long journey with her two children. They left Tibnīn not by train or motorcar, but as villagers had traveled for centuries: in a camel caravan that wound its way down toward Beirut on the Mediterranean coast. The road was dusty and slow, but each mile carried them farther from the only home the children had ever known and closer to the unknown world where their father was waiting.

When they reached Beirut, they boarded a cargo ship bound for Marseilles. In Marseilles, they would be checked for their health. Then they would take a train to Paris and from there to Cherbourg.

For a woman from a small Lebanese village, the stations, languages, and crowds must have felt overwhelming, yet the path forward was fixed: each ticket, each platform, one step closer to America and reunion.

On Hinnah's 27th birthday, April 10, 1912, they reached Cherbourg and the ship that would make their names part of history. They stepped onto the RMS Titanic as third-class passengers, traveling under ticket number 2650, which had cost £15, 4 shillings, and 11 pence—a very real fortune for a farming family.[2]

Third class was the least expensive way across the Atlantic, but even there, Titanic offered more space and better accommodations than many emigrants had previously known. Hinnah joined scores of other Lebanese passengers on board, part of a sizeable Arabic-speaking community within the ship's lowest decks.

Life at sea quickly took on a rhythm. In the crowded third-class spaces, Hinnah likely found comfort in familiar faces and shared language, trading stories with other families from Lebanon and the broader Middle East. At the same time, she had her hands full with Mariyam, 10, and Jirjis, 8, who, like many children on a long voyage, turned the ship into a playground. They ran along corridors, explored the corners of third class, and sometimes slipped into vacant cabins to hide, their laughter echoing off the steel walls as their mother hurried after them.

A Young Irish Laborer: The Individual Inside the Crowd

Not every steerage passenger traveled as part of a family. Many were young men traveling alone, drawn by wages and pushed by limited prospects at home. In Irish migration, this pattern had a long history: leave first, establish yourself, send money, bring others later—or never.

It is difficult to tell the story of every individual traveler in steerage with full specificity. Records exist, but personal documents do not always survive, and many lives left only thin traces. Still, the type matters because it was common: a young laborer with modest savings, a ticket paid through sacrifice, a pocket with a name and address written carefully, and the belief that hard work would translate into a future.

Traveling alone meant fewer responsibilities, but also fewer protections. In steerage, community could be improvised, but it was not guaranteed. If you were separated from your language group or companions, you navigated alone. If you misunderstood an instruction, no parent corrected it. If you missed the moment when a corridor opened or a line moved, you might not get a second chance.

Steerage was not only for families and children but also for the young workforce of migration: people who carried their future in their own hands and had no backup plan if those hands came up empty.

Daniel Buckley

Daniel Buckley was 21 when he boarded Titanic at Queenstown on Ireland's south coast, carrying more hope than luggage. He held a third-class ticket, number 330920, purchased for £7, 15 shillings, and 7 pence—a price that represented months of hard work for a farm family.[3]

His destination was not just "America" in the abstract, but a specific address and a pair of familiar faces: an uncle and aunt living on Tremont Avenue in New York, who had gone ahead and were now the anchors drawing him across the ocean.

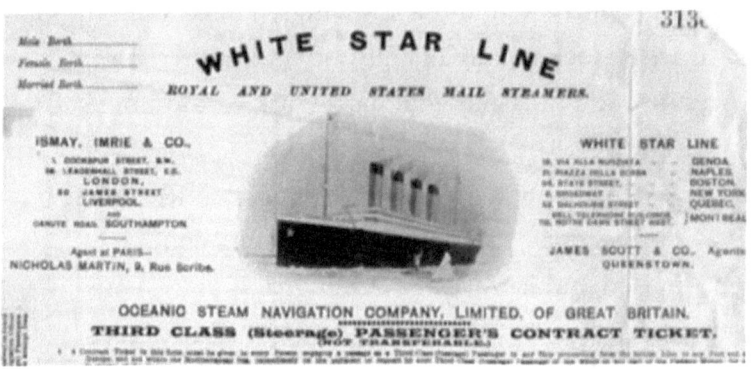

Born on September 29, 1890, in Boherbue, County Cork, Daniel was the eldest in his family and the one chosen—or volunteering—to go first.

As the ship lay at anchor off Queenstown, small boats ferried Irish passengers and their bundles out to the towering liner. Daniel found himself among dozens of fellow emigrants, many from rural backgrounds like his own, trading fields and lanes for steel decks and crowded dormitories below.

For Daniel, the voyage was more than a crossing of the ocean. It was a step from the narrow opportunities at home into the unknown sprawl of New York, where family waited on Tremont Avenue and where he hoped there would be steady work and a chance to send money back to Ireland.

As Titanic turned west and Queenstown faded into the mist, he carried his family's expectations and watched the horizon slip away.

Daniel Buckley

The Crew: Frederick Barrett

Titanic's 885 crew for the maiden voyage was 885 souls, and as was common at that time, they were not a permanent workforce. Most were casual workers who came and joined only hours before leaving Southampton.

This is the last known picture of RMS Titanic on the surface of the ocean. It was taken during her maiden voyage at Crosshaven, Ireland, just after the vessel departed Queenstown, where it had stopped before heading westwards towards New York. Public Domain.

If steerage passengers experienced Titanic as a system they entered, crew members experienced it as a system they kept running. Their work held the ship together in ordinary times—and shaped what happened in an extraordinary one.

Frederick Barrett, a fireman aboard Titanic, offers a rare view of the ship's lower operational world in the minutes after impact. The firemen and trimmers were not near the promenades or the wireless room. They were near heat, noise, vibration, and a brutal clarity: when water came where it should not, they were among the first to know.

Frederick Barrett

Frederick William Barrett spent his working life in the heat and darkness below deck, where most passengers never set foot. Born in 1883 in Bootle, near Liverpool, he grew up in a part of England where the docks and shipyards shaped the rhythm of everyday life. The sea offered work, and for a man like Frederick, that meant the stokehold—shoveling coal into the roaring mouths of a ship's boilers.

By 1903, he had joined the Cunard liner RMS Campania as a stoker, one of the many firemen who kept that great Atlantic steamer moving across the ocean. The work was exhausting and dirty, but steady, placing him at the heart of the new age of steam. In 1904, he left Campania for the Allan Line ship Parisian, and then for the White Star liner RMS Cedric, following jobs from company to company the way seamen and stokers often did, going where a berth could be found.

By the spring of 1912, Frederick was 29 and an experienced stoker, hardened by years spent before open furnace doors in the rolling bellies of big ships. On 6 April 1912, in Southampton, he was hired aboard the new White Star liner Titanic as a lead stoker, a position of responsibility among the firemen.

Lead stokers helped direct work in the boiler rooms, ensuring the furnaces were fired correctly and the pressure was steady for the engines above. Titanic, larger and more modern than most ships Barrett had served on, demanded an enormous amount of coal each day, and men like him supplied it by the shovel-load.

Joseph Bell — Chief Engineer

The Bell family had been yeoman farmers in the Cumbrian countryside for generations. Joseph Bell, the eldest child, was born in 1861 and was expected by many to follow the plow as his father had. Instead, as a young man, he left the fields behind and went to Newcastle, taking an apprenticeship as an engine fitter, trading hedgerows and stone walls for steel, rivets, and the pounding rhythm of machinery. The engine room, not the farmyard, would become his world.

By 1885, Joseph had joined the White Star Line and began a long career in the engine departments of its steamers, serving on vessels that ran to New Zealand and to New York. At sea, he learned every part of a liner's mechanical heart: how boilers were fired and cleaned, how engines were maintained on long voyages, how to balance power and fuel so a ship kept time without wasting coal.

Day to day, his work as an engineer meant long hours below the waterline, listening to the throb of pistons and turbines and reading the ship's health from steam gauges and temperatures rather than from the sky or the sea.

On shore, he built a different kind of life. In 1893, Joseph married Maud Bates in Ripley, and together they had four children. The pattern of those years was familiar to many seafaring families: months away at sea, responsible for the hidden power that kept great ships moving, broken by stretches at home when he was simply a husband and father, telling his children about faraway ports they might never see.

Professionally, his rise was steady. Around age thirty, he was promoted to Chief Engineer on the Coptic, a post of great responsibility. A Chief Engineer was the master of all mechanical operations on board: the boilers, engines, electrical generators, pumps, and all the systems that kept water moving, lights burning, and the ship herself alive. Under his authority were teams of engineers, electricians, boilermakers, and fitters, all of whom looked to him for orders, standards, and example.

Before Titanic, Bell served aboard Olympic, the first of White Star's new class of liners, and that experience gave him an intimate knowledge of how these vast ships behaved under power.

When he was transferred to Titanic, he "stood by" the ship during her construction and fitting-out in Belfast, watching as engines and boilers were installed, as systems were tested, and as the machinery that would later be his responsibility was brought to life. For a Chief Engineer, standing by during building meant learning the ship from the inside out—knowing every valve and pipe run, every pump, every boiler room layout, long before passengers ever set foot on board.[4]

Once Titanic entered service and Bell took his place as Chief Engineer, his working world lay deep below the passenger decks. His staff on the maiden voyage was substantial. Under him were twenty-five engineers in total, including himself, each assigned to different watches and different parts of the engine rooms and auxiliary machinery.

Joseph Bell

There were six electricians, among them Chief Electrician Peter Sloan, Second Electrician Alfred Samuel Allsop, and Electrician Boykett Herbert Jupe, supported by three assistant electricians. Two boilermakers were on hand to deal with repairs to the boilers and associated piping, along with a ship's plumber responsible for the maze of fresh-water, waste, and steam lines, and a clerk who kept the records—logs of pressures, temperatures, repairs, and coal consumption.

Day-to-day, Bell's responsibilities were both technical and human. He drew up and oversaw the engine-room watch schedule, ensuring that each boiler room and machinery space was adequately manned around the clock. He reviewed readings in the engine-room log, watching for any sign of trouble: a boiler that ran too hot, a pump that lost efficiency, or a bearing temperature that crept upward. He coordinated with the bridge, responding to telegraphs from the engine-room indicator—"Full Ahead," "Half Ahead," "Slow," or "Stop"—by directing his men to adjust the engines and throttle valves, making sure the great reciprocating engines and turbine responded smoothly.

The routine below deck was relentless. Firemen and trimmers labored at the furnaces, shoveling coal. At the same time, engineers walked their rounds, checking oil flows, listening for unusual vibrations, and making minor adjustments to prevent small problems from becoming serious failures.

Bell's job was to ensure that all of this ran as one coordinated system, hour after hour, day after day, whether the ship was easing out of harbor or driving hard across the open Atlantic.

While passengers above enjoyed the illusion of a floating hotel—warm, bright, and smooth—Joseph Bell knew how much work it took to maintain that sense of effortlessness.

His command lived in the heat, noise, and confined spaces far below, where coal dust and sweat were constant companions, and where there were no portholes to show the sea or sky. It was his responsibility to keep Titanic's heart beating steadily, to balance power and safety, and to be ready, at any moment, to answer whatever orders might come down from the bridge.

Reginald Lee

Reginald Robinson Lee — Lookout on Duty

Reginald Robinson Lee was twenty-nine years old when he signed on as a lookout aboard Titanic. He was not an officer, not a decision-maker, and not a man with authority over the ship's course or speed. His role was specific and narrow: to watch.

His world on Titanic consisted of a small circle of steel and wood high above the sea, and a single duty that filled every minute: to scan the horizon for danger.

He had not come to that perch by accident. Born in Benson, England, Reginald had already served his country at sea as an Assistant-Paymaster in the Royal Navy before retiring from that post in 1900. In the years that followed, he moved into the world of the big transatlantic liners, and by early 1912, he was serving on RMS Olympic, Titanic's near-twin and older sister ship. When Titanic was preparing for her maiden voyage, Lee was among the men transferred to the new liner and officially joined her crew on 6 April 1912.

A lookout's job on Titanic was simple yet demanding. The lookouts were posted in the crow's nest, a small sheltered platform partway up the foremast, well forward of the bridge, so the ship's structure would not block their vision.

From there, high above the bow, they scanned the dark line where sea met sky, watching for anything that might threaten the ship: other vessels, floating wreckage, sailing boats, or, in cold northern waters, ice. Their tools were basic. At night, they relied mainly on their eyes and ears, since bright lights would destroy their night vision and any sound above the wind—the wash of waves on something solid, a warning bell from another ship—might matter.

In normal conditions, the lookouts worked in pairs, taking turns on duty in set watches, with regular changes to keep them from becoming too tired or too numb to what they saw. The climb up to the crow's nest meant ascending the mast by an internal ladder or using access from the forecastle deck, then stepping into the narrow, cold enclosure where they would stand for their watch. Once in place, they moved very little. Standing or leaning on the rail, they swept their eyes across the horizon in slow, overlapping patterns, letting their gaze pass from directly ahead to either bow and then back again, trying not to fixate on any one patch of darkness too long.

Communication with the bridge was simple and direct. If the lookouts saw an object ahead that could be a hazard, one would strike a warning bell in the crow's nest—three sharp rings for something directly ahead, fewer for objects off the port or starboard bow. The other would grab the voice pipe or telephone connection that led down to the bridge and call the officer on watch, giving a brief, urgent report: what they had seen and where it lay relative to the ship.

After that, their responsibility ended; it was up to the officers below to decide how to proceed, whether to alter course, change speed, or hold steady.

The first three nights at sea had passed without incident. The days and nights blended into a routine: climbing to the nest, adjusting his eyes to the gloom, feeling the cold wind bite at his face as the ship drove westward through the Atlantic.

He and his fellow lookouts watched the water and the sky, reported lights and vessels, and returned to their quarters at the end of each watch, knowing they had done their part in a chain of safety that stretched from the engine rooms to the captain's bridge.

On the evening of 14 April, the air grew sharper as Titanic sailed into colder waters, but for a lookout, that was one more fact to note, not a cause for alarm.

At 11 p.m., Reginald Lee climbed again to his post in the crow's nest, taking over from Archie Jewell and George Symons together with his fellow lookout, Frederick Fleet. The ship beneath them was calm and steady, her engines driving her forward at nearly full speed through a sea that, by late night, had become unnervingly smooth. Above, the sky was clear and star-filled; ahead, the ocean was a dark, polished surface broken only by the faint white of the bow wave.

Somewhere ahead, beyond their straining eyes, the ship was already rushing toward the thing that would test every crew member whose story was about to be told.

[1] "Anders Johan Andersson," Encyclopedia Titanica.

[2] "Hinnah Tu'mah," Encyclopedia Titanica, passenger records for RMS Titanic, ticket no. 2650.

[3] "Daniel Buckley," Encyclopedia Titanica.

[4] "British Wreck Commissioner's Inquiry, testimony of Frederick Scott (Greaser, SS Titanic), May 10, 1912.

Chapter 4 — Day Three: April 14, 1912

"Colossus ship of the Titans, unsinkable beneath the stars,
Champagne popped too soon."

— Stewart Stafford

THE PUBLIC FACE OF Titanic was softness: carpeted stairs, polished brass, and white linen. But beneath that surface was an architecture of control and supervision. People moved when they were permitted to move. They learned quickly which corridors belonged to them and which did not. The ship did not need to shout its rules; it taught them through routine.

To a first-class passenger, a steward's presence was reassuring. He appeared at the right moment with a tray, a message, or a quick reply. The boundary lines were enforced quietly and continuously, through manners and customs. That is how class works when it is stable: it becomes a habit.

To those traveling in steerage, a steward's presence meant something different. There were fewer of them, their authority felt harsher, and their role was less about comfort than containment. Steerage was designed for efficiency—sleeping spaces were tightly packed, corridors were narrow, and public rooms were functional. Large numbers of people were packed into a limited space and expected to remain orderly, without the informal social pressure that kept first-class in line.

Recreation, 3rd-class dining area

Junior stewards and steerage staff were the daily interface between policy and people. They carried instructions, directed traffic, corrected behavior, and enforced movement rules that were not only about comfort but also about separation. The goal wasn't cruelty: it was to implement the system.

Titanic was built to keep classes apart for practical and commercial reasons: crowd control, ticket integrity, and sanitation concerns. That separation required constant maintenance.

The Rules of Movement

For steerage passengers, the ship was not a free space to explore. It was a controlled environment with boundaries that were often learned the hard way. People were redirected, and doors were closed. Certain stairways did not belong to them. Even when movement was technically possible, it was socially policed. A wrong turn could lead to an encounter with authority—brief, firm, and humiliating enough to discourage curiosity next time.

Over time, steerage passengers internalized this. They stayed where they were supposed to, and when the emergency came, the habit remained.

In a crisis, a first-class passenger who needed to reach the deck could move through familiar public spaces and follow the flow of people. A steerage passenger trying to do the same often had to override what the ship had been teaching them since the moment they boarded: don't go there. Rules that were merely inconvenient in daylight became dangerous at midnight.

Third-class passengers on deck, Public Domain

Information as a Privilege

Titanic also did not distribute information evenly. In first class, communication moved through a web of staff and proximity. Passengers overheard things. Stewards relayed messages. Officers were visible. The ship's official and unofficial information traveled faster because the people who mattered most to the company were concentrated in one area and served by the greatest number of staff. In steerage, information could arrive late, in fragments, or not at all.

Part of this was structural: fewer staff, more passengers, and less direct access to officers. Part of it was linguistic: steerage was multilingual, which slowed everything because every instruction became a two-step process when translation was needed.

This is where interpreters and bilingual passengers became critical. On Titanic, translation was not just helpful: it was an essential survival tool. A single person who understood English could turn noise into meaning and panic into direction. Without interpreters—formal or informal—steerage passengers were left to interpret tone, gesture, and rumor.

Steerage Matrons: Care and Containment

Steerage matrons existed in the space between welfare and discipline. On paper, their role was protective— monitoring conditions, assisting women, helping maintain decency and order in crowded spaces. In practice, the role also served the ship's deeper interest: keeping steerage passengers controlled.

A matron could calm an anxious mother, defuse conflict, and manage the daily friction of overcrowding. She could also discourage movement, enforce separation between men and women in certain areas, and keep steerage from spilling into areas the company did not want it to reach.

April 14, 1912

By the third day, Titanic had settled into itself. The novelty of departure had faded. The small anxieties of embarkation—finding cabins, learning routines, testing boundaries—had given way to repetition. For many aboard, especially in steerage and among the crew, ordinary was a reassurance. It meant the ship was doing what it was supposed to do, and that was calming to everyone.

Morning in Steerage

Morning in steerage began with sound before sight. The ship's low vibration never stopped, but people learned to sleep through it. What woke them instead were footsteps in the corridors, the movement of others rising, the distant clatter of service. Meals structured the day. Not because the food was remarkable, but because it provided the daily rhythm.

Steerage passengers ate at assigned times in communal spaces. The food was plain but filling—bread, porridge, soup, and meat when available. For families like the Anderssons, meals were one of the few moments when the day felt shared rather than fragmented. Children were gathered. Adults sat still. Conversation flowed in familiar languages. People talked about destinations. Winnipeg. Chicago. Minnesota. Addresses were repeated like incantations, as if saying the place often enough would make it real. Some compared notes on relatives already settled. Others listened more than they spoke, carrying their plans privately.

This was the work of waiting: imagining a future while time passed slowly.

Children at Play

Children adapted faster than adults. They learned which corridors were acceptable, which corners offered space to play, which adults tolerated noise, and which did not. They turned narrow areas into games, invented rules, and followed one another in clusters that shifted with both energy and occasional boredom.

For the Andersson children and others like them, the ship was already becoming a temporary world. The boundaries felt fixed, yet life went on within them. Laughter coexisted with uncertainty. Childhood did not pause for migration. Children at play were a visible sign of normalcy, and their presence reassured adults that things were as they should be. A ship with playing children did not feel like a ship in danger.

For eight-year-old Jirjis Tu'mah, the voyage with his mother and older sister, Mariayam, was nothing short of wondrous. Years later, he would remember the thrill of that journey: the gleam of the great ship, the vastness of its decks, and the hum of life echoing through every corridor. Inside, the polished wood and shining brass seemed magical to a boy seeing such a vessel for the first time.

Together, he and Mariayam roamed the passageways in wide-eyed delight, exploring empty cabins, whispering discoveries to each other, and racing up and down the staircases from one deck to the next as if they belonged to a floating world all their own.

By the third day at sea, the Andersson children, too, had made the great ship their own small kingdom. Ebba, Ellis, Ingeborg, and Sigrid, ranging in age from 5 to 11, had learned which corridors echoed, which staircases led to windy decks, and which corners offered the best view of the endless water. They laughed at the gulls trailing the ship and pressed their noses to the railings, trying to spot a fish leaping in the waves below.

The older girls took pride in showing their younger siblings the places they had found — a quiet bench near a lifeboat or a spot just outside the dining room where they could feel the engines' hum beneath their feet. Even little Sigvard, age 2, toddled on the 3rd-class deck under his mother's watchful eye, clapping at the sound of the ship's horn.

By evening, their cheeks glowed from the sea wind, and as the ship's lights flickered to life, the children grew still, listening to the low rhythm of the ocean — a sound that would soon come to feel like the heartbeat of their adventure.

Anna Nysten

Anna Sophia Nysten had boarded Titanic as just one of many young women among the hundreds of Scandinavian emigrants who filled the third-class spaces below decks.[1]

She was traveling with the Andersson family, not as kin but as something just as common in steerage—a familiar adult presence, another pair of hands, and a helper. In the first days after departure, life settled into a routine shaped by the calm sea, the steady hum of the engines, and the days passing marked by meals, conversations in Swedish, and the constant movement of children underfoot.

As a single woman in third class, Anna Sophia's world was informal but constrained. The ship's design and White Star Line rules discouraged unaccompanied wandering between classes, and steerage passengers largely remained within their own public rooms and open deck areas. She would have slept in a shared cabin, risen early, and spent much of her time in the communal spaces—corridors, dining saloons, and the well decks where families gathered for air and light. These were crowded spaces, alive with voices, babies crying, boots scraping on steel. Privacy was rare; familiarity unavoidable.

Within that closeness, roles emerged naturally. Anna Sophia likely helped Alfrida Andersson with the children—watching them, steadying them on the stairs, and keeping them occupied during long hours at sea. Such arrangements were common: women shared the labor of caring for infants, mending clothes, translating when needed, and passing along news. For a single woman, usefulness offered both purpose and belonging. The work filled the hours and anchored her in the small social world of her traveling companions.

Above all, these early days were defined by anticipation. Conversations turned to America—jobs were rumored, relatives waited, futures were imagined but not yet real. Anna Sophia would have stood at the rail when weather allowed, watching the Atlantic stretch endlessly ahead, the ship carrying her away from what was known and toward something untested. Like so many in third class, she was not traveling for comfort or adventure but for possibility. The ship moved steadily westward, and with it, the fragile hopes of those below decks who, for the moment, believed the hardest part of the journey was already behind them.

Daniel Buckley

Daniel Buckley had spent the first few days orienting himself—learning where he was permitted to go, when meals were served, and how the ship expected him to behave.

He slept in a shared steerage compartment with three other young men, surrounded by other single men and families. Space was tight but not chaotic. Bedding was assigned. Luggage was stowed. Meals arrived at set times, served plainly but sufficiently. Bread, soup, porridge, and tea. Nothing to linger over, but enough to establish rhythm.

He had settled into the routine shared by many young, single men in steerage: spending time on the open deck when permitted, leaning against railings, watching the sea, and smoking if he had tobacco. Conversations were practical. Where are you going? Who are you meeting? What work are you hoping for?

Irish steerage passengers often clustered naturally, drawn by accent and familiarity. Talk would have drifted between optimism and restraint. There was time to kill, and little to do with it. Some men slept more than usual. Others walked the same short routes repeatedly. Children ran past. Families gathered. Buckley was alone, but not isolated.

By the 14th, Titanic felt reliable.

Nothing had gone wrong. The ship ran smoothly. Meals came when expected. Crew moved through steerage with routine authority. The separation between classes felt less like restriction and more like routine.

Sunday Evening

By Sunday evening, dinner would be semi-routine for the passengers in third class. Served at the usual hour, eaten in long rooms that echoed with conversation and the scrape of benches. That night's menu offered rice soup, roast beef, sweet corn, and bread. Dessert was plum pudding and tea. The passengers lingered slightly longer than they might have earlier in the voyage. There was no sense of hurry. The ship had proven itself steady. Tomorrow would be another day of waiting.

Families began preparing children for bed as they had each night since departure. Coats were folded. Shoes were lined beneath bunks. Mothers washed faces with cold water and smoothed hair already familiar with the ship's routines. Children were tired in the particular way children become tired at sea—restless one moment, heavy-limbed the next.

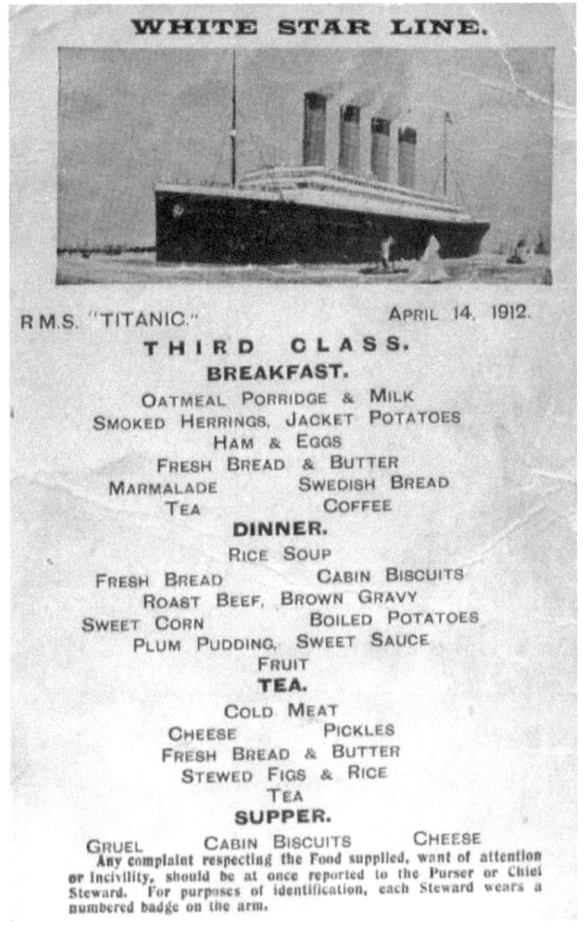

WHITE STAR LINE.

R.M.S. "TITANIC."   APRIL 14, 1912.

THIRD CLASS.

BREAKFAST.

OATMEAL PORRIDGE & MILK
SMOKED HERRINGS, JACKET POTATOES
HAM & EGGS
FRESH BREAD & BUTTER
MARMALADE   SWEDISH BREAD
TEA   COFFEE

DINNER.

RICE SOUP
FRESH BREAD   CABIN BISCUITS
ROAST BEEF, BROWN GRAVY
SWEET CORN   BOILED POTATOES
PLUM PUDDING, SWEET SAUCE
FRUIT

TEA.

COLD MEAT
CHEESE   PICKLES
FRESH BREAD & BUTTER
STEWED FIGS & RICE
TEA

SUPPER.

GRUEL   CABIN BISCUITS   CHEESE

Any complaint respecting the Food supplied, want of attention or incivility, should be at once reported to the Purser or Chief Steward. For purposes of identification, each Steward wears a numbered badge on the arm.

Titanic Menu

In steerage, bedtime came earlier than it did above. Darkness fell faster below decks, and the ship's rhythms encouraged sleep. Corridors quieted gradually, not all at once. A lullaby hummed here. A prayer whispered there. The sound of engines filled the spaces between voices.

For families like the Anderssons and the Tu'mahs, the night was about containment—gathering everyone into the small space assigned to them, keeping children close, keeping the future intact for one more night. Whatever uncertainty waited across the Atlantic could be postponed until morning.

For single men like Daniel Buckley, the evening passed differently. After supper, he would have returned to his compartment or, if permitted, stood briefly on deck, watching the light fade from the water. Cold crept in quickly, and the sea offered no landmarks to hold the eye. Below, bunks waited.

By the time Buckley lay down, the ship was already quieting. Conversation thinned. Boots were removed. The long work of waiting gave way to sleep. The crossing, so far, had taught him nothing that suggested tonight would be different from the nights before.

The ship moved steadily through the dark.

Above them, officers monitored the night. Lookouts took their posts. Engines drove the ship forward with confidence. And the last ordinary evening aboard Titanic slipped into history—quietly, without announcement, carrying hundreds of people into sleep who did not yet know that routine had reached its end.

Below Decks: The Crew's Day

While steerage passengers marked time by meals, the crew marked it by shifts.

Below decks, the ship never rested. Firemen and trimmers worked in rotations that blurred the line between day and night. Coal was hauled, shoveled, and burned in relentless cycles. Heat pressed in and sweat-soaked clothing. The air was thick and metallic.

For men like Frederick Barrett and his fellow firemen, the ship's smooth progress was proof that the work was being done correctly. Engines running well meant no attention from above. No attention meant safety, wages, and continuation.

Off-shift, crewmen washed when they could, ate quickly, and slept deeply. There was little romance in the work. There was pride, sometimes, but mostly endurance.

Above them, lookouts rotated through long watches. Their work was quiet, exposed, and monotonous. Hours passed, scanning water that rarely changed. On Day Three, there was nothing remarkable to report. The ocean was calm. Visibility was good enough. Ice warnings had been received, but they did not alter the feel of the day.

The Chief Engineer's World

For the chief engineer and his team, Day Three was measured in systems. Steam pressure. Electrical output. Mechanical balance. The ship's success was invisible to passengers because success meant nothing went wrong. Lights worked. Heat flowed. Engines responded.

A well-run liner made labor disappear. Passengers were meant to feel carried, not supported. The cost of that illusion was paid in work below decks—work that continued regardless of weather, class, or expectation.

On Day Three, the system held.

When the night came, it came to a ship that felt secure in its patterns. And when those patterns broke, the people who had learned to wait would be the ones who lost the most time.

The Lookout Takes His Watch

For Reginald Robinson Lee, the evening of April 14 began the way many others had—without ceremony.

As a lookout, his day was structured by watches, not by meals or daylight. Titanic's lookouts worked in pairs in the crow's nest in 2-hour shifts, then had 4 hours off before going back on duty. During that day and night, Alfred Evans and George Hogg were on duty between 12 and 2 and between 6 and 8; Archie Jewell and George Symons were on duty between 2 and 4 and between 8 and 10; and Frederick Fleet and Reginald Lee were on duty between 4 and 6 and between 10 and 12.

At 10 p.m., Frederick Fleet and Reginald Lee took over from Archie Jewell and George Symons.[2]

The ship was calm. The sea was calm. In the cold, Frederick and Reginald climbed the nearly 50 feet to the crow's nest. Frederick stood on the port side of the crow's nest while Reginald stood on the starboard side.[3] High above the waterline, the world narrowed to horizon, starlight, and darkness. From the crow's nest, Titanic felt less like a ship and more like motion itself—forward, steady, uninterrupted.

There was no moon. The sky was clear, the stars sharp. The ocean lay unusually smooth, its surface offering little contrast.

Crows Nest, Titanic

The absence of binoculars—a detail later seized upon— was not something Lee could remedy. It was not his decision and not within his authority. And they may not have mattered anyway. He scanned the sea as generations of sailors had before him, relying on eyes trained to detect shape and movement in darkness.

Below him, the ship carried thousands who had already gone to bed. Officers maintained course. Around him, the Atlantic offered nothing that distinguished danger from emptiness. Minutes passed. Then more minutes. Reginald continued to scan the horizon.

When the shape finally appeared and the night broke its silence, Reginald would do precisely what the system asked of him.

He would see.

He would alert.

And the rest would unfold beyond his control.

[1] "Anna Sofia Nysten," Encyclopedia Titanica.
[2] British Wreck Commissioner's Inquiry, testimony of Frederick Fleet and Reginald Lee (Lookouts, SS Titanic), May 9–10, 1912.

Chapter 5 – Fire and Ice

"Nature, to be commanded, must be obeyed."

— Francis Bacon

Fire

BEFORE TITANIC EVER TOUCHED open water, it carried a problem below decks. Fire.

Eight days before departure from Southampton, a coal fire had ignited in one of the ship's coal bunkers, located between boiler rooms 5 and 6.[1] Additionally, one of the watertight bulkheads ran through the center of the bunker, with coal on either side.

The fire was neither an explosion nor a visible blaze but a slow, dangerous coal fire, heating and smoldering under pressure. Such fires were not unheard of on steamships. Coal could ignite spontaneously when stored in large quantities, especially if air circulated unevenly through the bunker.

A coal bunker fire was a serious concern, but it was not worrisome enough to cancel the sailing. These fires were typically fought internally—by removing burning coal, spreading it out, starving it of oxygen, and feeding it into the boilers to eliminate the hazard.

That solution came with a cost. It required manpower and time: for firemen to work harder, longer, and under worse conditions than usual. And it meant the fire had to be managed continuously, not extinguished at once.

The Firemen's Work

Shortly after leaving Southampton, fireman Frederick Barrett received orders to empty the coal bunker in boiler room 6. A fire had been discovered there.

Titanic before leaving Southampton; the circled area contains a dark area believed to be the fire in the coal bunker. Public Domain.

For the men working below decks, the fire added more heat, smoke, and exhaustion to the already brutal labor. They worked in rotating shifts, shoveling coal into furnaces in temperatures that could exceed 100 degrees. The bunker fire added another task to that routine: identifying compromised coal, moving it safely, and keeping the fire from spreading deeper into the ship's structure.

This was not heroic work in the popular sense. It was dirty, repetitive, and relentless. Firemen were not celebrated for preventing disaster. They were expected to absorb risk quietly so that the ship above could proceed normally.

Joseph Bell's Decision

Responsibility for managing the fire fell under the engineering department, ultimately supervised by Chief Engineer Joseph Bell and his senior staff.

The decision to proceed with the voyage while managing the fire was not reckless in the context of the time. It was an industrial judgment shaped by precedent, pressure, and confidence in the crew's ability to control the situation.

Ships sailed with coal fires before, and crews had contained them before. Delays were costly—financially, reputationally, and logistically. There is no evidence that officers above the engineering chain were fully briefed in detail, nor that passengers were informed. The fire was treated as a technical issue, not a navigational one.

And so Titanic sailed, the fire still active when she left port.

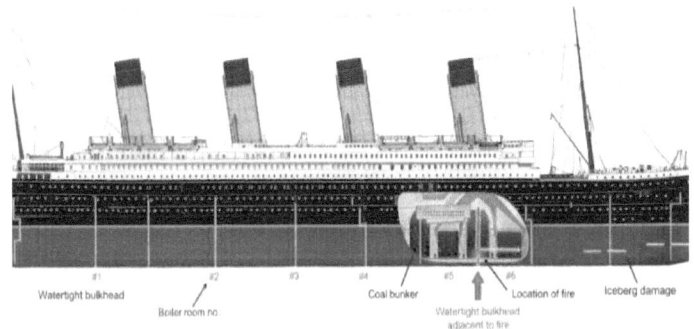

Diagram of coal bunker fire and Iceberg damage

The work of putting out the fire lasted until Saturday, April 13th. Upon inspection, Frederick Barrett later testified that the bulkhead was fire-damaged from top to bottom, with the lower half warped aft and the upper half warped forward.[2]

While the fire's ultimate role in the disaster is debated, it does mean that the voyage began without margin. It meant stress was already present in the ship's industrial core and that men below decks were already fighting a threat long before the night of April 14th.

And when the collision came, those same men—already exhausted, already working under abnormal conditions— would be asked to do more.

Ice

The first sign of danger came quietly on the morning of April 14, 1912. At 9:00 a.m., the wireless room aboard RMS Titanic received a message from the RMS Caronia: reports of "bergs, growlers, and field ice" drifting in their path.[3] Captain Edward J. Smith read the warning carefully, acknowledged it, and pressed on. The North Atlantic could be treacherous in spring, but ice reports were familiar enough; a seasoned captain could navigate through them safely—or so it seemed.

By early afternoon, the messages became more frequent and more uneasy. At 1:42 p.m., RMS Baltic passed along a note from the Greek steamer Athenia: she too had seen "icebergs and large quantities of field ice." Smith again acknowledged the report and, this time, brought it to the attention of J. Bruce Ismay, chairman of the White Star Line, who was enjoying the prestige of Titanic's maiden voyage. After a brief consultation, Smith ordered a new, more southerly course to steer clear of the worst of the ice.[4]

Only minutes later, at 1:45 p.m., another message arrived—this one from the German liner SS Amerika, sailing not far to the south. She had passed "two large icebergs." But the bridge never heard the message. The reason was fateful yet straightforward: the Marconi wireless transmitter aboard Titanic had broken down the night before, and the two overworked radio operators, Jack Phillips and Harold Bride, had spent the night repairing it. In the rush to resume sending passengers' personal messages, this vital alert was apparently overlooked or misplaced.[5]

As evening fell, other ships continued to send warnings. At 7:30 p.m., SS Californian reported "three large bergs." At 9:40 p.m., another message arrived, this time from the SS Mesaba: "Saw much heavy pack ice and great number [of] large icebergs. Also field ice." It was, by any standard, a grave warning. But that message, too, never reached Captain Smith. Jack Phillips, buried under a backlog of private telegrams, was transmitting passenger messages to the Cape Race station in Newfoundland. Preoccupied, he set the Mesaba's warning aside.

At 10:30 p.m., Cyril Evans, the wireless operator from the Californian, sent a final, direct warning: his ship had come to a full stop, surrounded by ice fields only a few miles away. But when his message interrupted the stronger signals from Cape Race that Phillips was handling, he snapped back, "Keep out; shut up, I'm busy." Evans complied—and turned off his set for the night.

Despite the steady stream of reports, Titanic steamed ahead at 22 knots, nearly her top speed. Slowing down in icy waters was not the practice of the day; captains relied on their lookouts and the watch on the bridge to spot danger in time.

As Fifth Officer Harold Lowe later explained, "The custom was to go ahead and depend upon the lookouts... to pick up the ice in time to avoid hitting it."[6]

That night, the lookouts did their best. But the sea was glassy calm, the moon absent, and the bergs showed no white surf against the darkness—only silence, vast and cold, waiting. By the time the Titanic's crew finally saw the ice ahead, it was far too late.

11:39 p.m., April 14, 1912, Atlantic Ocean

Frederick saw it first. He immediately rang the crow's nest bell three times, then moved to the starboard side of the crow's nest and picked up the telephone to inform the officers on the bridge. Sixth Officer Moody picked up the phone and asked what they had seen.

"Iceberg right ahead," he replied.

"Thank you," said James.

James relayed the warning to First Officer William Murdoch, who had the con at the time. From that point, the response was procedural—compressed into seconds: Murdoch moved to the telegraphs and the wheel commands. The orders were meant to do two things at once: turn the ship and reduce forward drive.

Murdoch ordered a hard turn. The practical intent was clear: swing the bow away from the hazard as fast as possible. Quartermaster Robert Hichens, at the wheel, put the helm over.

Murdoch also ordered engine changes through the telegraphs—intended to slow the ship and help the turn take effect. Exactly which engine orders were sent, and whether "full astern" was used, varies in testimony; what does not vary is that the bridge attempted to check speed immediately.

Almost simultaneously, Murdoch also activated the system to close the watertight doors—a rapid, centralized action designed for precisely this kind of emergency. The doors were meant to seal off lower compartments before flooding could spread.

All of this happened within a narrow window of seconds. In an attempt to slow the ship, Joseph Bell and his engine crew were ordered to stop or reverse the engines (accounts vary).

They complied.

Frederick Barrett was on duty in boiler room 6 at 11:39 p.m. He was talking to the second engineer, John Henry Hesketh, when the red light and bells sounded, signaling the order to stop the engines. He shouted to the men in the boiler room to shut the dampers and the doors to the furnaces, and to shut off the wind for the fires.[7]

Impact

Then came the sensation that made the warning real: not a crash like a ship hitting a wall, but a prolonged, cold interruption, a shudder and scrape along the starboard side that many would later describe as strangely muted.

On the bridge, those six seconds registered as vibration and resistance—an event you could feel more than hear. Captain Edward Smith was summoned and arrived shortly after the collision. The ship did not stop abruptly. The bridge's immediate task was not evacuation, but assessment: What had been struck? How extensive was the damage? Could the ship continue?

That meant sending word below, receiving reports back, and watching the ship's response—trim, speed, and the early signs of flooding.

In those first minutes, the bridge was not yet running an evacuation. It was trying to understand the scale of the wound.

Frederick Barrett and the firemen working in Boiler Room No. 6 understood the severity of the damage almost immediately. The impact tore open the ship's starboard side, and seawater poured in with force, flooding the space within moments. Frederick forced his way through the watertight door into Boiler Room No. 5, but an order came quickly: he was to return.

By the time he did, water was already rising rapidly— eight feet deep in Boiler Room No. 6. The engineers moved to the pumps, attempting to slow the inevitable. At the same time, alarms carried through the machinery spaces. Orders followed in quick succession. The engine room signaled for stokers to abandon their posts and make for the deck.

Frederick began to withdraw again, but was stopped once more—this time ordered to remain in Boiler Room No. 5. Even there, the sea was not far behind. Water was already forcing its way in, spreading through the compartments faster than the men below could contain it.

Illustration, Titanic striking the iceberg

As the water rose quickly in the boiler rooms, Joseph Bell was already moving toward the bridge when he met Bruce Ismay at the top of the B Deck staircase. Ismay asked him directly whether he believed the ship had been seriously damaged. Bell did not minimize the situation. He told Ismay the damage was severe but added that he hoped the pumps might keep the flooding under control.[8]

There was nothing more to say. Ismay turned and returned to his cabin, while Bell continued on toward the bridge. The exchange was brief, factual, and unfinished — an assessment offered in motion, before the scale of the injury had fully declared itself.

The Lookouts

Frederick Fleet and Reginald Lee stayed at their posts until 12 am, twenty minutes after the collision. During that time, no general alarms were sounded or public announcements made. Stewards had not yet been ordered to wake anyone. There was no rush toward the lifeboats. In the wireless room, operators had not yet sent distress calls. That decision would come later, when uncertainty hardened into inevitability.

The ship still appeared stable. In the first and second classes, most passengers remained in the lounges or cabins, unaware that anything more than a minor incident had occurred.

Below levels, however, the situation was clear.

The carpenter began sounding the ship, measuring the rate of flooding. Reports from the forward compartments grew steadily worse. One by one, the limits of the ship's design were being reached — and exceeded.

But for now, Titanic remained a functioning ship with a serious problem.

Above, officers calculated.

Below, men fought the water.

And between those two realities, thousands of passengers slept through the most critical minutes of the night. By then, the ship's fate was already sealed.

[1] British Wreck Commissioner's Inquiry, Report of a Formal Investigation into the Loss of the S.S. Titanic, evidence of Frederick Barrett, fireman, day 18, questions 13,590–13,600 (London: HMSO, 1912).

[2] British Wreck Commissioner's Inquiry, testimony of Frederick Barrett (Leading Fireman, SS Titanic), May 9, 1912.

[3] "Titanic in Belfast," Titanic History, Facts and Stories (archived January 6, 2021).

[4] Jay Henry Mowbray, The Sinking of the Titanic (1912).

[5] Jeremy Hsu, "How Marconi's Wireless Tech Helped Save Titanic Passengers," MSNBC, April 17, 2012 (archived January 6, 2021).

[6] https://en.wikipedia.org/wiki/Sinking_of_the_Titanic

[7] Jack Winocour, The Story of the Titanic as Told by Its Survivors (New York: Dover Publications, 1960), 253–54.

[8] Barrie B. Hodgson and Brian Freer, Tramp to Titanic: Life and Times of Joseph Bell Chief Engineer (1st ed.; UK: Clearline Assistance, 2013).

Chapter 6 — Orders in the Dark

"The tide rises, the tide falls; the twilight darkens, the curlew calls."

—Henry Wadsworth Longfellow

HINNAH TU'MAH HAD ALREADY put her younger son, Jirjis, to bed, but she remained uneasy. Her daughter, Mariyam, had not returned, and Hinnah stood waiting at the door of their cabin, listening for footsteps in the corridor.

It was there that the ship jolted.[1]

The sudden impact threw the door against her, slamming it into her hand with enough force to injure her. As she attended to the pain, several men passed through the corridor to see what had happened. When they returned, they told her the ship was in danger, but that they had been instructed to remain in their cabins and pray.

Hinnah did not wait.

She dressed Jirjis quickly and began moving upward through the ship, guided at points by crewmen. When she reached the boat deck, she left her son near a lifeboat and turned back immediately, returning alone to the steerage quarters to search for Mariyam.

She had barely reached the corridor outside her cabin when she saw her daughter emerging from a nearby vacant room, where she had been sleeping.

There was no time to question it.

Hinnah didn't waste a moment and, with clear and quick thinking, gathered what she could—including the paper with her destination address in the United States. As they moved into the passageways, Hinnah noticed a gate being locked behind her, cutting off the route they had just passed through.

She did not stop.

When she returned to the boat deck, Jirjis was still where she had left him.

Illustration, Hinnah Tu'Mah

The Andersson Family and Anna Sophia Nysten

No one recorded the Anderssons' final movements.

They left no testimony. No one survived to be interviewed. Their names appear in the passenger lists and in the death records, and then they disappear into the silence that surrounds so many third-class families.

The later testimony of Anna Sophia, their traveling companion, offers only a glimpse of what transpired belowdecks.

"We had gone to bed," she recalled, "but I'm not sure I was asleep. The first thing I distinctly remember was a terrific jar and a sound such as one hears when the bottom of an automobile scrapes the ground as you drive on a deep-rutted road. That was the ship striking the iceberg."[2] She dressed, didn't panic, and made sure she had enough supplies of food and clothes with her, which she carried in a basket. Somebody advised her to put on a lifejacket.

But still, there was no cause for alarm. The stewards had advised them to stay put. Some were told the ship had merely struck ice and that there was no cause for concern. Others were instructed to dress warmly and wait. Information was sporadic and incomplete, and it offered different accounts of what was transpiring above. The language was calming, not urgent. For a family with five children, that mattered.

Preparing children to move at night through unfamiliar corridors was not simple. It required time. Shoes had to be found. Coats located. Younger children to be carried or calmed. Parents had to decide whether to wake everyone at once or wait for clearer instructions.

Waiting was the habit the ship had taught.

As the minutes passed, steerage corridors grew more crowded. Confusion increased unevenly. Some families heard rumors. Others heard nothing at all. Language barriers slowed understanding. Information arrived in fragments, translated imperfectly, or not translated at all.

What is clear from survivor testimony is that movement from steerage did not begin all at once. It came in waves — some families guided upward early, others much later, and some not at all.

For families traveling together, staying together was often the priority. Parents resisted separating from their children. Mothers resisted leaving their sleeping sons or daughters behind. Fathers delayed their movement as they tried to gather everyone into one group. The logic was human and fatal: survival was imagined as collective, not individual.

As water spread through the lower decks, the ship's design became an obstacle rather than a guide. Routes that had been unfamiliar in daylight became nearly impossible at night. Gates were closed and opened in sequence as the crew attempted to manage the flow. Some families reached stairways only to be redirected. Others turned back, hoping to find another way.

It is also true that many gates were routinely locked at night. Tragically, these constraints slowed the progress of many third-class passengers as they struggled toward the

Boat Deck. Geography worked against them. Their cabins lay far below the upper decks, and the path upward was long, confusing, and poorly marked. Compounding the problem, members of the crew—some still uncertain themselves about the severity of the situation—often failed to communicate any real sense of urgency.

By the time Anna and the Andersson family finally emerged onto the upper decks, the clock was nearing 1:30 a.m. The lifeboat operation was already well underway. None of the Anderssons survived. That fact alone places them among the many third-class families for whom delay—measured in minutes, misunderstood instructions, and the long climb from below—proved fatal.

Their story was not unusual, and that is what makes it devastating.

Daniel Buckley

Daniel was asleep in a communal third-class cabin near the bow when the collision took place. He awoke to find seawater ankle deep on the floor.

"I heard some terrible noise and I jumped out on the floor, and the first thing I knew my feet were getting wet; the water was just coming in slightly. I told the other fellows to get up, that there was something wrong and, that the water was coming in. They only laughed at me. One of them says: "Get back into bed."[3]

He didn't listen.

Daniel dressed hurriedly as his three bunkmates stirred and began to rise. The cabin was small and crowded, and once they were awake, he stepped out into the corridor to wait. As he stood there, two crewmen passed, shouting a warning as they went: "All up on deck unless you want to get drowned!"

Now he did not hesitate. He moved upward at once, never seeing his bunkmates again.

In the communal areas, he noticed other passengers already wearing life jackets and realized he had left his behind. He turned back toward his cabin to retrieve one, but was forced to stop. Water was already rising in the stairway, reaching the third or fourth step. The route was no longer passable.

Eventually, he gathered with a group of other third-class men near a short flight of stairs leading into a first-class area. One man attempted to go up, but a crewman arrived, pushed him back, and slammed the gate shut, locking it. The man, furious, chased after the crewman and broke the lock, later saying that had he caught him, he would have thrown him into the sea.[4]

Daniel followed.

On his way upstairs, he encountered a first-class passenger who had two life jackets. The man gave Daniel one and helped him secure it properly. With that, he made his way to the boat deck. There, he later stated, he assisted in lowering five lifeboats until nearly 1:30 a.m.

Evacuation and Lifeboats

The official evacuation had begun just after midnight.

At 12:05 a.m., the illusion of comfort aboard Titanic began to unravel. Captain Edward Smith gave the order to uncover the lifeboats and muster the passengers, preparing them for an emergency. Passengers were waking in their cabins, puzzled by the sudden silence: the steady throb of the engines and the faint vibration through the decks had stopped, leaving an uneasy stillness in their place.

Smith also ordered that distress calls be sent at once. In the wireless room, Jack Phillips and Harold Bride took down the position calculated by Fourth Officer Joseph Boxhall and began tapping out distress signals into the night. Boxhall's estimate, hurriedly made in the confusion, placed Titanic on the west side of the ice belt and was off by about 13.5 nautical miles.[5]

Without any loudspeaker system to rely on, stewards now had to spread the word the hard way. They went door to door along the passageways, knocking, calling, and entering cabins to wake sleeping passengers and crew. They told them to dress warmly, put on their lifebelts, and make their way up to the boat deck. How thorough this muster was significantly depended on a passenger's class.

First-class stewards had only a handful of cabins to manage, and many personally helped their charges into coats and lifejackets before escorting them to the deck. In the second and third classes, where each steward was responsible for many more people, there was little time for such attention. Doors were flung open, lights switched on, and brief instructions shouted: Get your lifebelts on, go up top.

In third class, especially, families and single travelers were often left to find their own way after being told to come on deck. Narrow corridors, unfamiliar layouts, and language barriers added to the confusion. Many passengers and even some crew members hesitated. Some refused to believe anything serious was wrong with such a grand, "unsinkable" ship; others did not want to leave the warmth and bright lights inside for the freezing, black air outside.

No official announcement told them plainly that the ship was sinking. A few observant souls noticed that the decks had taken on a slight list, tilting almost imperceptibly, but most clung to the hope that this was only a precaution.

Around 12:15 a.m., the tone grew more insistent. Stewards began ordering passengers to put on their lifebelts, yet many still did not grasp how grave the situation was. On the forward well deck, where chunks of ice lay scattered from the impact, some younger passengers kicked and tossed the broken pieces around, turning them into makeshift footballs. For a few surreal minutes, it felt like a strange midnight game rather than the beginning of a disaster.

Up on the boat deck, officers and crew were wrestling with the practical problem of saving lives. Titanic carried only 20 lifeboats: 16 wooden boats slung on davits along the sides of the ship—eight on each side—and four collapsible boats with wooden bottoms and canvas sides.

The collapsibles were stored upside down, with their sides folded in, and had to be set up correctly before being dragged to the davits for lowering. Two were tucked under the wooden lifeboats, and the other two were lashed on top of the officers' quarters, high and nearly out of reach. Each of those heavy craft weighed several tons and would have to be manhandled down to the boat deck, costing precious time.

On paper, the lifeboats could each carry up to 68 people. Altogether, if every seat were filled, they could hold 1,178 souls. It sounded like a large number until set beside the reality: more than 2,200 people were on board. Even if everything went perfectly, there was room for barely half of those now being shaken awake in the quiet, slanting corridors of the great liner.

Joseph Bell and the Work of the Engineers

From midnight onward, Joseph Bell's world narrowed to systems.

By then, the collision had become a flooding problem measured in compartments and minutes. Joseph and his senior staff focused on keeping the ship operational as long as the machinery spaces remained workable: maintaining steam where possible, keeping pumps running, and preserving electrical power and lighting as long as the ship's internal layout allowed.

Later accounts attribute his remark—"My God, we're doomed!"—after he learned that water was overcoming the ship's internal barriers and moving aft. Whether he said those exact words is difficult to prove, but the underlying reality is not in doubt: by the early hours, the engineering department understood that the flooding could not be controlled.

Even so, the engineers continued to work.

There is a version of the Titanic story that has become almost fixed in public memory: the band on deck, the music holding steady as the night worsens; the lights still burning in windows as the ship angles downward. Whether true or partly constructed after the fact, some men chose to remain where duty placed them.

Music on deck required a deck that could still function. Lifeboats could be lowered only in the dark if crews could still see what they were doing. The ship's internal communications, pumps, and electric lighting depended on machinery still turning below. The lights did not stay on by sentiment. They stayed on because men in the engine and boiler rooms kept them on—feeding boilers, maintaining steam, and holding the electrical plant as long as the sea allowed.

Whatever one believes about the band's final minutes, the broader truth is more complicated and less cinematic: Titanic remained operational longer than it had any right to, and that bought time—real minutes—for people to find their way upward and for boats to be lowered.

But Joseph and most of the engineers remained below, never abandoning their posts and working until the end. However, later testimony recounted that at least some engineering personnel were eventually released to go on deck, but by then, nearing 2 a.m., the lifeboats were gone. A small group of engineers was last seen on the starboard side near the electric crane, standing together on the boat deck.

Joseph Bell was last seen also around 2:00 a.m. attempting to reach the bridge by telephone—seeking confirmation, instruction, or simply an updated picture of what the ship was doing above. No reply came.

By then, the ship's fate was no longer a question of engineering. It was a question of time.

And in those final minutes, time belonged to the sea.

12:45 am to 2:05 a.m.

Lifeboat 7 was launched at 12:45 a.m. with 28 people on board. Lifeboat 6, on the port side, was the next to be lowered at 12:55. It also carried 28 people, including the "unsinkable" Margaret "Molly" Brown and movie star Dorothy Gibson. The first two lifeboats were primarily composed of first-class passengers – men and women – and three crew members.

Conditions were now dire. Two engineers, Herbert Harvey and Jonathan Shepherd, died in boiler room 5 when, around 12:45, the bunker door connecting to No. 6 collapsed, sweeping them away by "a wave of green foam," according to leading fireman Frederick Barrett, who barely escaped.

Lifeboats were sent down from the davits every few minutes on both sides of the ship, yet many left with far fewer people than they could safely carry. Boat No. 5

pulled away with only 41 people aboard, No. 3 with 32, No. 8 with 39, and the small emergency boat No. 1 with just 12 people in spaces meant for 40.

The evacuation was chaotic, and people were injured as they tried to escape. One woman slipped into the gap between lifeboat No. 10 and the ship's side, only to be grabbed by the ankle and safely returned to the promenade deck before she made a second attempt. In another incident, first-class passenger Annie Stengel suffered several broken ribs when a German-American doctor and his brother leaped into Boat No. 5, landing on her and knocking her unconscious.

Even once in the boats, the danger was not over. Lifeboat No. 6 was nearly swamped by water gushing from the ship's side as it went down, but still managed to get clear. Boat No. 3 narrowly avoided catastrophe when one of the davits jammed during lowering, leaving the passengers briefly at risk of being thrown into the sea before the problem was cleared.

From 12:55 to 1:10 a.m., four lifeboats—Nos. 1, 3, 6, and 8—were launched carrying only first-class passengers and crew. Lifeboat 1 left with 12 occupants, Lifeboat 3 with 35, Lifeboat 6 with 24, and Lifeboat 8 with about 30 people. It was not until 1:20 a.m. that Lifeboat 9, the first to carry third-class passengers, was lowered away.

From 1:20 a.m. to 1:45, finding a lifeboat became increasingly urgent. The boat deck was now a crush of movement and noise.

The bow was settling lower, the list more pronounced, and officers were trying to impose order on something rapidly slipping beyond control. Lifeboat 9 went next, swinging out over the black water with a mix of women, children, and a handful of men from second and third class, along with crew at the oars. It left with just over forty people, though later survivors from other boats were transferred into it until more than seventy crowded its thwarts.

Nearby, Lifeboat 10 dropped away almost alongside, carrying around fifty-five passengers—mostly women and children from second and third class who had finally come up from the lower decks, herded by a few determined crew, including third-class steward John Edward Hart.[6]

Only minutes later, at about 1:25, the pace quickened. Boats 11 and 12 were loaded and lowered one after the other, officers shouting to hurry as the deck tilted and the emergency rockets burst overhead. Lifeboat 12 went down with just over forty people, many of them third-class women and children mixed with a few men and stewards.

Lifeboat 11 was packed more tightly—around seventy souls—so full that people were pressed shoulder to shoulder on the wooden benches as she dropped toward the sea, the ship's massive hull towering beside them.

Around 1:30, Lifeboat 14 was launched, close to capacity with about sixty passengers and crew. The scene around it was fraying at the edges now: some men tried to push forward, others hung back in disbelief, and officers shouted "Women and children first!" over the roar of escaping steam.

By 1:35, two more boats—16 and 15—were being worked at the davits almost at once. Lifeboat 16 went down with roughly fifty-six aboard, a heavy mix of second and third-class women and children, and a thin scattering of crew to row.

Lifeboat 15 was one of the most crowded to leave, crammed with around seventy-one people as it dropped— women and children jammed together, with just enough seamen to handle the oars.

Some boats still had empty spaces; others, like 15, rode perilously low in the water, so overladen that any sudden movement might have swamped them. At about 1:40, Collapsible C was brought to the davits and hastily filled with forty-seven people—mostly first-class women and children, a few men, and crew—its canvas sides hurriedly raised as it was lowered away. The air was full of shouted orders, crying children, and the relentless hiss and boom of vented steam.

By 1:45 a.m., Lifeboat 2, one of the small emergency cutters, was being lowered under Fourth Officer Boxhall's charge. It left with barely two dozen aboard, about twenty-five or twenty-six people in a boat built for more. As it pulled away into the darkness, the great ship's bow was far lower than it had been only twenty-five minutes earlier. In that short span, a rush of boats had gone down from both sides—some under-filled, some dangerously crowded—while hundreds of passengers still milled on the slanting decks, only beginning to understand that the lifeboats were running out and time was almost gone.

In steerage, the scene was unfolding differently. Leading Fireman Charles Hendrickson later recalled looking down the third-class corridors and seeing groups of steerage passengers clustered with their trunks and bundles, standing as if waiting for orders that would never come. This learned, stoic passivity was shaped by generations of being told to obey social superiors rather than to act on their own.

One of the surviving third-class men, August Wennerström, recalled the same scene in the dining saloon: hundreds of third-class passengers gathered in a great circle around a preacher, praying, crying, and begging God and Mary for help, yet making no move to escape. "They lay there and yelled," he wrote, "never lifting a hand to help themselves," as if their will had drained away and they were waiting for heaven to decide their fate.

The last boat launched was Collapsible D, which left the ship at 02:05 with 25 people. As it was being lowered, two more men jumped onto the boat. The seawater was now at the boat deck.

SS Californian

Earlier that night, the steamer SS Californian had sent Titanic a warning about heavy ice ahead. Captain Stanley Lord, wary of driving his slower ship into the vast field of drift ice, ordered Californian to stop at about 10:00 p.m. and wait for daylight before attempting to work through it.

By 11:30 p.m.—just ten minutes before Titanic struck the iceberg—Californian's sole wireless operator, Cyril Evans, shut down his set and turned in for the night. On the bridge, Third Officer Charles Groves noted a large ship off the starboard bow, ten or twelve miles away. He watched as it turned sharply to port, then appeared to stop, hanging in the darkness. In the years that followed, investigators would revisit that moment again and again, arguing that had Evans stayed at his post for even fifteen more minutes, he might have heard the Titanic's distress calls—and altered the fate of hundreds.

A little more than an hour after Evans left the wireless room, Second Officer Herbert Stone saw five white rockets arc upward from the silent ship and burst against the night sky. Unsure whether they signaled celebration or danger, he reported the sighting to Captain Stanley Lord in the chartroom, where uncertainty, rather than urgency, governed what came next. No orders were given to proceed through the ice or close the distance. Stone, increasingly uneasy, confided to a colleague, "A ship is not going to fire rockets at sea for nothing," sensing that something was badly wrong out there in the dark.

Lifeboat 13

When Titanic began to founder, lookout Reginald Lee was ordered to man Lifeboat 13, where he helped Hinnah Tu'mah and her two children inside.

Fireman Reginald Barrett later testified that he made his way up through a hatchway and reached the starboard

94

side of A Deck when only two lifeboats remained. He boarded Lifeboat 13 as it was being filled. The boat was crowded—Reginald recalled nearly seventy people aboard, far exceeding the anticipated capacity.

Anna Sophia Nystem, finally on the upper deck with the Andersson family, remembered the scene: "Of course, the women and children were put into the boats first, but several men tried to get in them too. It was sad, the way families were separated."

In Lilly Setterdahl's *Not My Time to Die – Titanic and the Swedes on Board*, the author states that Anna and the Anderssons thought they were all "going down together" when a sailor pushed Anna into Lifeboat 13.

Daniel Buckley was standing nearby when a rush of men —passengers and crew —jumped into it. In a moment that left no time for reflection, Daniel followed, leaping in with them. Shortly afterward, two officers arrived with a crowd of third-class passengers and ordered the men out. Most complied. When the officers finished, only Daniel and five other men remained aboard, including firemen and crew.

Believing he would be removed, Daniel broke down and began to cry. A woman in the boat took pity on him, threw her shawl over his head, and told him to keep still. The ruse was enough. The officers did not notice him. As they were being lowered from the starboard side, another lifeboat, Lifeboat 15, descended above them. For a moment, it seemed as if it would come down directly on top of them.

Only at the last instant was the descent halted, checked just in time to prevent the two boats from colliding.

Lifeboat 13 then pulled away.[7] It was 1:43 a.m.

Lifeboat No. 15 being nearly lowered onto lifeboat No. 13, depicted in an illustration by Charles Dixon

[1] Leila Salloum Elias, The Dream and Then the Nightmare: The Syrians Who Boarded the Titanic, the Story of the Arabic-Speaking Passengers (Atlas, 2011).

[2] "Anna Sofia Nysten," Encyclopedia Titanica.

[3] Senan Molony, The Irish aboard Titanic (Dublin: Wolfhound Press, 2000)

[4] "Daniel Buckley," Encyclopedia Titanica.

[5] British Wreck Commissioner's Inquiry, Report of a Formal Investigation into the Loss of the S.S. Titanic (London: HMSO, 1912).

[6] Nic Compton, Titanic on Trial: The Night the Titanic Sank, Told Through the Testimonies of Her Passengers and Crew (London: Adlard Coles, 2012), 297.

Part III—Aftermath

Chapter 7 — Rescue

"To live is to suffer, to survive is to find some meaning in the suffering."

— Viktor Frankl

BY ABOUT 2:00 A.M., the ship's angle had become unmistakable. The bow was deep underwater, and the stern had begun to lift, drawing the ship upward and out of balance. Objects that had stayed put now slid. Machinery shifted. The deck sloped sharply enough that standing required effort. For those still aboard, gravity became a warning.

Inside the ship, the limits of structure were being reached.

As the forward section was pulled down, stresses concentrated amidships. The hull—designed to flex, but not to bend beyond a certain point—began to fail. Somewhere beneath the surface, the ship broke apart. Those on deck felt it as a shudder, a release, a sudden change in motion rather than a single dramatic crack.

At approximately 2:18 a.m., the lights went out.

The electrical systems finally failed, plunging the ship into darkness. The bow disappeared completely beneath the surface, pulling the broken forward section away and leaving the stern briefly afloat, isolated and vertical against the night sky.

For a moment, the stern seemed to hesitate.

Then, at around 2:20 a.m., it began its final descent. Water rushed over the decks. Air escaped in bursts. The last visible section of Titanic slid beneath the surface of the Atlantic, and the sea closed over it.

The ship was gone.

What remained were lifeboats scattered across the dark water, debris spreading outward, and the sound—carried farther than sight ever could—of thousands of people suddenly left with nothing between themselves and the cold but the ocean itself.

The crossing was over. The waiting had ended.

A pocket watch retrieved from the wreck site, which stopped at 2:28

As Lifeboat 13 pulled away, Anna Sophia Nysten turned and saw the Andersson family standing together on deck. She watched the confusion unfold on the decks and later recalled hearing cracking noises as the ship went under.

Hinnah and the other survivors watched people jump or fall from the ship in their final moments. She tried to shield her children's eyes from the unfolding events by covering them with her cloak.

"The ship began to sink, and the deck was full of people. You can imagine how it looked. I can hardly describe it. Oh, how horrible it was when everything went dark," Anna wrote to her mother later. "When the ship went down, we were not far away, and we were almost sucked under."

April 15, Monday

In the early morning hours of April 15, help was already moving through the dark.

Illustration of Titanic's final moments

RMS Carpathia had received Titanic's distress calls after the signals were sent by Titanic's operators, Jack Phillips and Harold Bride. Carpathia immediately altered course and drove hard through ice fields, pushing her engines beyond their normal limits to reach the reported position as quickly as possible.

By approximately 4:00 a.m., Carpathia arrived at the scene.[1]

RMS Titanic was gone. In her place lay a scattered field of lifeboats drifting in the cold Atlantic, the sea calm but filled with debris and survivors clinging to what remained. The first lifeboat was brought alongside shortly after Carpathia's arrival, and rescue began at once.

Through the early morning, Carpathia worked steadily, boat by boat, hauling survivors aboard—many suffering from exposure, shock, or injury. Crew members distributed blankets and hot drinks, and makeshift medical spaces were set up to tend to the most severe cases. The work was methodical, urgent, and quiet.

At 8:30 a.m., when the last lifeboat had been recovered and no further survivors could be found, Carpathia turned away from the wreck site. With all those she could save now aboard, she set her course westward toward New York City, carrying with her the living remnants of a ship that no longer existed.

Aboard Carpathia

The first moments aboard Carpathia were not only moments of relief, but also of shock.

Survivors came up the ship's sides stiff with cold, hauled from lifeboats that had held them for hours in the dark. Many could not stand without assistance. Some were barefoot. Others still wore nightclothes soaked with seawater. Nearly all were silent.

Collapsible lifeboat D photographed from the deck of Carpathia on the morning of 15 April 1912

Blankets were passed down immediately—thick, rough wool, wrapped around shoulders and heads. Hot drinks followed: tea, coffee, and soup. The warmth came slowly. Hands shook. Faces stared without focus.

Daniel Buckley recalled the simple sequence: being helped up, given a warm blanket, and being asked who he was. There was no celebration, no sense of escape yet— only the mechanical process of being received.

Names were recorded.

Crew members and volunteers wrote them down carefully, sometimes asking twice, sometimes spelling phonetically when accents made clarity difficult. Survivors were asked where they had come from, which lifeboat they had been in, and whether they were alone or with someone else.

For many, that question was the hardest to answer.

Some hesitated, unsure whether the people they were looking for were alive or merely late. Families, separated in the darkness, searched faces instinctively as each new group arrived: scanning for children, spouses, and siblings—hoping, even now, for a miracle.

Anna Sophia recalled: "You can imagine how happy we were to see the steamer Carpathia close in on us and we could come aboard. They were so good to us. We received blankets and coffee and brandy as much as we wanted. But there was still much groaning and crying because most of us had lost a dear relative. It was hardest for those who had lost family members. Many became hysterical."

Daniel described being taken below, given dry clothing, and directed into a space already crowded with others. Public rooms had been converted quickly—chairs pushed aside, floors cleared, passengers from Carpathia surrendering cabins, coats, and comfort without protest. Daniel's mother later received this letter from her son:

On board the Carpathia, 18 April 1912:

Dear Mother,

I am writing these lines on board the Carpathia, the ship that saved our lives. As I might not have much time when I get to New York, I mean to give you an account of the terrible shipwreck we had.

At 11 p.m. on the 14th, our ship Titanic struck an iceberg and sank to the deep at 2.20 a.m. on the 15th. The present estimation is 1,500 lost, 710 saved. Thank God some of us are amongst the saved.

We had a great time on the Titanic. We got a very good diet and we had a very jolly time dancing and singing.

We had every type of instrument on board to amuse us, but all the amusement sank in the deep. I will write a note when I get to New York. Good-bye at present.²

Shock manifested unevenly. Some survivors spoke rapidly, recounting events in fragments. Others said nothing at all. A few wept openly, but many could not yet cry. The mind lagged behind the body, unable to absorb what had happened in the space of a single night.

What united them was exhaustion.

They had survived the cold, the waiting, the fear of the sea—but now, safe for the first time, their bodies began to fail them. People fell asleep sitting upright. Others stared at the walls until they were gently guided elsewhere.

Inside, the work was repetitive and careful: blanket, drink, name, space. Again and again. Each arrival adding weight to the truth no one yet said aloud—that survival had not been evenly distributed, and that for many, rescue had come too late. And the quiet, disorienting realization that the ship that had carried them into the Atlantic was gone.

Seven hundred and five souls boarded the Carpathia. Nearly 1,500 had perished at sea.[3]

Who Survived, Who Did Not

But those 1500 lives were not evenly distributed. Roughly 62% of first-class passengers survived, compared with about 41% in second class. Just 25% of third-class passengers survived. Class determined proximity to information, access to open decks, and time. Those differences became decisive in the final hours.

Colorized illustration of the iceberg thought to have been hit by Titanic, original photograph was from the morning of 15 April 1912. Note the dark spot just along the berg's waterline, which was described by onlookers as a smear of red paint thought to be of a ship.

Two-thirds of women and children did survive, but the most considerable losses of women and children were in third class. Only one in five men survived. The "women and children first" practice—applied unevenly and imperfectly—nonetheless shaped who lived and who did not.

Chaos in the Numbers: The First Reports

In the hours immediately following Titanic's sinking, a fog of confusion descended over the exact count of survivors. The wireless messages that crackled between ships and shore stations painted a wildly inconsistent picture, one that would take days to clarify.

The first wireless message reporting Titanic's distress came from the Carpathia at 1:40 AM on April 15th, stating simply: "Titanic struck iceberg, sinking fast." But it was the messages that followed, carrying conflicting survivor counts, that would create a rollercoaster of hope and despair for waiting families.

At 6:44 AM, a message from the Olympic reported optimistically that "All Titanic passengers safe." This false report, picked up by several newspapers, sparked premature celebrations in New York and Southampton. By afternoon, the Associated Press was reporting that Titanic was being towed to Halifax with all passengers safe - another cruel piece of early misinformation.

The Carpathia's wireless operator, Harold Cottam, worked tirelessly sending lists of survivors, but the task was overwhelming. Names were misspelled, particularly those of immigrant passengers. Some survivors gave different names than those on the passenger list, either out of confusion or fear. Third-class passengers, many speaking little or no English, had particular difficulty making their presence known.

The White Star Line offices in New York posted and revised survivor numbers throughout April 15th and 16th:

8:00 AM, April 15: "All passengers saved"

2:00 PM, April 15: "675 saved, mostly women and children"

6:00 PM, April 15: "866 rescued"

9:00 AM, April 16: "705 survivors confirmed"

The confusion was compounded by several ships in the area receiving fragmentary wireless signals. The SS Frankfurt, SS Mount Temple, and RMS Baltic all reported different versions of events and varying survivor counts. The Baltic's captain even reported seeing Titanic still afloat at 10:50 AM on April 15th - a ghost signal that gave false hope to many.

Particularly heartbreaking were the scenes at the White Star Line offices, where families gathered desperately seeking information. Third-class families faced additional challenges as many of their names were mangled in wireless transmissions or omitted entirely from early reports. The wireless operators, working with limited technology and overwhelming message traffic, prioritized the names of first-class passengers in their transmissions.

It would not be until April 18th, when the Carpathia finally docked in New York, that a definitive count would emerge: 705 survivors out of 2,224 passengers and crew. The confusion of those first days, however, had already seared itself into the public consciousness, becoming part of the tragedy's lasting legacy.

Arrival in New York

When the Carpathia finally docked at Pier 54 in New York on April 18th, 1912, the stark divisions of the Titanic continued to play out on American soil. The reception of survivors laid bare the social hierarchies that had shaped every aspect of the disaster.

A Tale of Two Arrivals

First-Class Reception

As the Carpathia approached the pier, private cars and luxury hotels had already arranged for their wealthy clients. The Waldorf-Astoria, the Ritz-Carlton, and other prestigious establishments sent representatives to meet first-class survivors. John Jacob Astor IV's widow, Madeleine, was whisked away in a private limousine, while other elite passengers found refuge in the homes of New York's social elite.

The press eagerly sought interviews with first-class passengers, whose stories dominated newspaper headlines. Molly Brown, Bruce Ismay, and other prominent survivors received immediate medical attention from private physicians. Their accounts of the disaster were recorded in detail and preserved for history, with their names and experiences carefully documented.

Colorised photo of Ned Parfett, "Titanic paperboy" outside the White Star Line offices at on Cockspur Street near Trafalgar Square in London. April 16, 1912. Public Domain.

Second-Class Reception

Second-class passengers faced a more modest but still organized reception. Aid societies and religious organizations had arranged temporary accommodations at mid-range hotels. Many found assistance through their professional connections or religious affiliations. Their stories, while less prominently featured than those of first-class passengers, still made their way into newspaper accounts.

Steerage: The Forgotten Survivors

For steerage survivors, arrival in New York meant facing yet another round of immigration procedures. Many were detained at Ellis Island despite their traumatic experience. Without money, contacts, or English-language skills, they struggled to navigate the aftermath of the disaster.

The disparity in treatment extended to financial assistance. While first-class passengers received immediate aid and compensation, steerage survivors often struggled to access basic relief funds. Many immigrant survivors, having lost everything in the disaster, faced the challenge of starting over in America with nothing but the clothes they wore when rescued.

The Hebrew Immigrant Aid Society, the Irish Emigrant Society, and other immigrant assistance organizations worked tirelessly to support these survivors. They provided temporary housing in boarding houses and settlement homes, but resources were stretched thin. Many steerage survivors slept on cots in charitable facilities or church basements.

Language barriers complicated their ability to tell their stories or seek help. While wealthy survivors gave interviews from hospital beds or hotel suites, many steerage passengers couldn't convey their experiences to the English-speaking press.

When recorded at all, their accounts were often filtered through interpreters or aid workers.

The Crew's Reception

The surviving crew members faced their own challenges. While officers were treated similarly to second-class passengers, most of the 214 surviving crew members were given passenger cabins on the Red Star Line's steamer SS Lapland. Many were quickly sent back to England, their stories untold and their trauma unaddressed.

The Lost Voices

The White Star Line's offices were flooded with telegrams and visitors seeking information about survivors, yet the company's responses reflected the same class distinctions. Inquiries about first-class passengers received prompt attention, while families seeking information about steerage passengers often waited days for any news.

This segregated reception foreshadowed how the disaster would be remembered. The stories of wealthy passengers would fill history books and shape the public narrative, while the experiences of steerage passengers and crew members often faded into obscurity, preserved mainly in immigration records and aid society documents.

Many of Titanic's surviving passengers did not remain in New York but continued their journeys to destinations across the country.

Charities were set up to help survivors and their families, many of whom had lost their sole wage earner or, in the case of many third-class survivors, everything they owned. In New York City, for example, the American Red Cross disbursed financial aid to survivors and dependents of those who died.

[1] Walter Lord, A Night to Remember (New York: Henry Holt and Company, 1955), 188–195.

[2] "Irish Daniel Buckley and the Titanic," IrishCentral.

[3] Dave Gittins, Cathy Akers-Jordan, and George Behe, "Too Few Boats, Too Many Hindrances," in Samuel Halpern, ed., Report into the Loss of the SS Titanic: A Centennial Reappraisal (Stroud, Gloucestershire: The History Press, 2011).

Chapter 8 — Inquiries, Legacy, and Lost Voices

"Believe those who are seeking the truth. Doubt those who find it."

— André Gide

WITHIN HOURS OF CARPATHIA'S arrival in New York, two nations began preparing for what would become the most extensive maritime investigations of their time. The parallel inquiries - one American, one British - would reveal not only the circumstances of Titanic's sinking, but also the deeply rooted problems in the shipping industry itself.

American Investigation

The American investigation that Senator William Alden Smith of Michigan launched was conducted with unprecedented speed, beginning just one day after Carpathia docked.

At the elegant Waldorf-Astoria Hotel and later in the Senate Office Building, Smith assembled a remarkable collection of witnesses: surviving officers, crew members, passengers from all classes, and shipping company officials.

The American hearings quickly exposed the challenge of cross-class testimony. While officers and first-class passengers testified in relative comfort, crew members and steerage survivors faced a more difficult experience. Many crew members, still in shock and wearing borrowed clothes, were aggressively questioned about their actions during the disaster. Language barriers complicated matters further—several immigrant survivors required interpreters, and their testimony was often truncated or misunderstood.

Second Officer Charles Lightoller emerged as a key witness, though his measured responses suggested a man walking a fine line between truth and loyalty to the company. When questioned about the ship's speed despite ice warnings, Lightoller's answers were notably evasive. "It was common practice," he repeated, though Senator Smith pressed him to say whether it was safe.

The British Board of Trade Inquiry

While the American investigation was still ongoing, the British Board of Trade launched its own inquiry under Lord Mersey.

Beginning on May 2, 1912, at the Scottish Drill Hall in London, this investigation took a markedly different approach. Where the American inquiry had been broad and sometimes sensational, the British hearings were technical and focused.

The contrast in how witnesses were treated was striking. Officers received respectful questioning and were addressed by their titles. Crew members, particularly those from steerage areas, faced more skeptical treatment. Several crew members later reported feeling intimidated by the formal atmosphere and legal proceedings.

The testimony of lookout Frederick Fleet proved particularly powerful. Fleet's statement that he had no binoculars in the crow's nest - they had been left behind in Southampton - highlighted the casual approach to safety equipment. When asked if binoculars might have helped spot the iceberg sooner, Fleet's simple "Yes, sir" echoed through the hall.

Key Findings and Contradictions

Both inquiries reached similar core conclusions, differing only in emphasis. The overall conclusion was clear: the sinking was not an unavoidable act of nature but the result of human decisions layered one upon another.

The American inquiry found that Titanic maintained excessive speed despite repeated ice warnings, entering known ice fields as if schedule and prestige outweighed caution. Ice was treated as an inconvenience rather than a condition demanding restraint, and the ship paid for that confidence with torn steel and time fatally compressed.

The investigation also exposed deep structural failures in preparedness. The ship carried lifeboats for barely half those aboard, a deficiency that was legal under existing regulations but indefensible in practice. Emergency procedures were poorly defined and inconsistently communicated; crew members had not drilled together for a full-scale evacuation, and confusion reigned as orders varied from deck to deck.

Wireless operations, though technologically advanced, were inadequately staffed and poorly coordinated.

Distress messages were delayed, ignored, or misunderstood, narrowing the window for rescue.

Perhaps most damning was the inquiry's finding that class divisions shaped survival. Access to boats, information, and assistance was not equal across the ship. While some third-class passengers were physically prevented from reaching the boat deck, others were delayed by locked gates, unclear routes, or language barriers.

The inquiry concluded that the loss of life was exacerbated not only by mechanical failure and maritime negligence, but by a social order that persisted even as the ship went down—one that valued order, hierarchy, and appearances over urgency and human life.

The British Wreck Commissioner's Inquiry (the Mersey Report, issued 30 July 1912) framed the disaster as the predictable outcome of a modern liner being handled as if the old rules still applied. It concluded that the disaster was "brought about by the excessive speed at which the ship was being navigated." It criticized the standard navigation practice of pressing on through reported ice rather than reducing speed and treating an ice field as a condition requiring extraordinary caution and vigilance.[1]

On the ship itself, the inquiry did not rule that Titanic was inherently defective in her build; instead, it emphasized the limits of contemporary design assumptions—how watertight subdivision, though advanced, still had boundaries that the iceberg's damage exceeded. The report's recommendations pushed for more substantial safety margins in construction and equipment going forward.

Where the report was most cutting was on readiness: boat drill habits, crew preparation, and the regulatory complacency that left a ship carrying lifeboat capacity for only a portion of those aboard because the rules allowed it.

Wireless, too, was exposed as a system with modern power but old protocols. The inquiry dealt with practicalities—how wireless was staffed and used, and how distress and ice information could fail to move with the urgency the situation demanded—leading to calls for tighter expectations around wireless vigilance and procedure so warnings and emergencies could not be lost in routine traffic.

Impact on Maritime Safety

The findings did not remain ink on paper. They led to sweeping changes in maritime safety regulations and hardened into an international safety regime designed to prevent a single ship's choices from becoming a mass grave again.

In 1914, governments convened the first International Convention for the Safety of Life at Sea (SOLAS) to establish minimum standards for construction, equipment, and operation across national boundaries. One of SOLAS's clearest responses to the Titanic was arithmetic, not rhetoric: ships were expected to provide lifeboat accommodation for everyone aboard.

Alongside that came the insistence that help could not depend on chance listening—continuous watch on distress and safety frequencies became the expectation, and radio vigilance became part of the safety system rather than a commercial convenience.

The ocean itself was also put under watch. The International Ice Patrol, operating from 1914 onward, institutionalized what had been improvised and unreliable: coordinated iceberg surveillance and warnings for North Atlantic shipping lanes. Onboard, the new requirements evolved into regular emergency training and drills—not just for the crew but also for passengers, with musters expected early in a voyage—so an evacuation would be a practiced procedure rather than first-time chaos.

Time to get busy by Fisher, 1912. Public outrage at the disaster led politicians to impose new regulations on the shipping

Design and operations shifted in parallel, though not always as a single, universal mandate. After Titanic, ships were retrofitted and redesigned with stronger subdivision assumptions—bulkheads were extended higher on some vessels, double-bottom protection was expanded, and emergency systems (lighting, signaling, life-saving equipment standards) became central engineering considerations rather than optional upgrades.[2]

And while laws cannot erase social prejudice overnight, the post-Titanic reforms advanced a simple principle: in an emergency, procedures must be clear, well-drilled, and applicable to everyone on board—because the sea does not recognize class, language, or status. However, it would take decades for this principle to be fully implemented.

The Fading of Faces: How Steerage Was Erased from Memory

While the inquiries were underway in America and Britain, another event was unfolding between them in the icy Atlantic waters—the recovery of bodies.

When the scale of the disaster became undeniable, the recovery of the dead was entrusted to corporate and administrative decisions, which were once again shaped by class.

The cable ship CS Mackay-Bennett was dispatched along with several other Canadian vessels, each stocked with embalming supplies, undertakers, and clergy. What

123

followed was not a neutral humanitarian operation, but a triage that reflected whose lives—and bodies—were deemed worth preserving.

The Mackay-Bennett reached the wreck site first and was immediately overwhelmed. Bodies outnumbered supplies. Faced with limited embalming materials and strict health regulations that barred the return of unembalmed remains to port, the ship's captain and undertakers made a consequential decision: priority would be given to preserving the remains of first-class passengers.

The justification was practical on its face—wealthy victims needed to be visually identified to settle estates—but its effect was unmistakable. Dozens of third-class passengers and crew were committed to the sea, their bodies deliberately left unrecovered. In death, as in life, class dictated treatment.

The process was methodical. Recovered bodies were numbered, measured, and cataloged. Clothing, physical features, and personal effects were logged with care. The purser locked away the valuables. But the system itself required choices. Clothing was sometimes used to classify bodies as crew. Burial at sea was framed as a sailor's fate—an acceptable end—but this rationale fell almost exclusively on those with the least social standing aboard.

Those bodies deemed worthy of return were transported to Halifax, where an extraordinary bureaucratic effort followed. A temporary morgue was established in a curling rink. Officials built detailed identification systems. Families traveled from across North America to claim their dead. About two-thirds of recovered bodies were identified. The rest—unclaimed and unnamed—were buried under numbered markers.

Most of those graves lie today in Fairview Lawn Cemetery. Of the 333 bodies recovered—only about one in five of the more than 1,500 who died—the majority interred there were third-class passengers and crew. Their headstones bear numbers, not names. The markers are uniform. The lives beneath them were not.

Even in the final weeks, the pattern held. Bodies recovered later—drifting hundreds of miles from the wreck or retrieved from lifeboats like Collapsible A—were often buried at sea without ceremony. The last body recovered, a ship's steward, was numbered and buried quietly in Halifax. By June, search vessels reported that life jackets were deteriorating, releasing bodies to sink beyond reach. The ocean was closing over the evidence.

For many in third class, there was no return home, no funeral attended by family, no name carved in stone. Even their bodies were not considered worth the effort of bringing back.

The end of recovery marked the start of another subtle yet systematic erasure. While the stories of wealthy passengers were preserved in exhaustive detail, the narratives of those in steerage faded almost immediately, creating a distorted legacy that endured for decades.

The Press and Public Memory

In the days following the disaster, newspapers devoted countless columns to profiles of first-class passengers. The New York Times ran detailed accounts of the Astors, the Strauses, and other prominent figures. But steerage passengers, when mentioned at all, were often reduced to numbers or nameless groups: "immigrants," "foreigners," "third-class passengers." Their individual stories, dreams, and sacrifices were largely ignored.

The rare exceptions usually involved heroism that served the upper classes. When steerage passenger Eugene Daly helped several first-class women into lifeboats, his story made the papers, though even then some accounts misspelled his name or confused his nationality.[3]

The Language of Loss

Even the vocabulary used to describe the dead revealed the class divisions. First-class passengers were "lost," while steerage passengers were "drowned." Wealthy victims were "claimed by the sea," while poor ones "went down with the ship." These subtle linguistic differences reinforced the notion that some lives - and deaths - mattered more than others.

Memorials and Monuments

Physical memorials to Titanic's dead tell an equally stark story. In Southampton, where many crew members lived, the memorial lists officers by name but refers to most crew members simply as "crew." In Halifax, where many victims are buried, the gravestones of first-class passengers feature elaborate inscriptions and family histories. Steerage passengers, if identified at all, often have only numbers or basic names.

The Belfast memorial, erected in the city where Titanic was built, listed initially only the names of prominent passengers and crew. It wasn't until 2020 that a supplementary plaque was added acknowledging the steerage passengers who died - a belated recognition of this historical oversight.

Missing Names

The disparity in documentation created lasting gaps in the historical record. While detailed biographical information exists for nearly every first-class passenger, many steerage passengers remain poorly documented. Name changes after immigration, language barriers, and inadequate record-keeping have left some identities forever uncertain.

Some examples of this documentation disparity:

First Class: 98% of passengers fully documented with photos and biographies

Second Class: 75% with basic biographical information

Steerage: Less than 50% with verified full names and backgrounds[4]

The Preservation of Objects

Even in museums, this disparity persists. Artifacts from first-class cabins - china, jewelry, furniture - were carefully preserved and displayed. But few objects from steerage survived, and even fewer were deemed worthy of preservation.

In recent years, efforts have been made to rectify this historical imbalance. Genealogists and historians have worked to reconstruct the stories of third-class passengers, and projects such as the Titanic Heritage Trust have focused explicitly on documenting third-class passengers and crew members.

Digital databases now aim to tell the complete story of everyone who sailed on the Titanic, regardless of class. Yet the century-long gap in documentation leaves many stories incomplete or lost entirely. The erasure that began in 1912 created historical blind spots that can never be fully corrected.

[1]British Board of Trade, Report into the Loss of the RMS Titanic (1912).

[2] Daniel Allen Butler, Unsinkable: The Full Story of the RMS Titanic (Mechanicsburg, PA: Stackpole Books, 1998).

[3] "Eugene Patrick Daly," Encyclopedia Titanica.

[4] John P. Eaton and Charles A. Haas, Titanic: Destination Disaster (New York: W. W. Norton & Company, 1996).

Chapter 9—After the Waves: Lives Reshaped by Survival

"Flickering images faded with age, frozen thoughts hovering precariously in dead space, a whirlwind of memories that slice through my soul."

— Tahereh Mafi

THE PHYSICAL RESCUE FROM Titanic's icy waters marked only the beginning of a much longer journey for survivors. The disaster's impact would echo through their lives for decades, reshaping futures in vastly different ways depending on their social class and circumstances.

For crew members, the economic aftermath proved especially harsh. Many found themselves essentially blacklisted from maritime employment, particularly those who had testified critically at the inquiries.

Sarah Roth, a third-class passenger traveling to America to marry her fiancé, faced a different kind of struggle. Like many immigrant survivors, she had lost her documents when the ship went down. The American immigration authorities initially threatened to deport her, deeming her a potential public charge because of her lack of funds and papers. It took weeks of appeals and the intervention of immigrant aid societies before she was officially admitted to the country.[1]

The psychological trauma manifested in various ways. Harold Lowe, Fifth Officer, would wake in the night, hearing phantom distress calls. In steerage, many survivors struggled alone with their memories, with no access to psychological support. Nightmares, anxiety, and what we now recognize as PTSD became constant companions.

Support networks emerged, though they too reflected the ship's class divisions. Immigrant survivors created their own informal support systems within their communities. In New York's Lower East Side, a group of Jewish survivors met regularly at a local synagogue, sharing their experiences in Yiddish and helping each other navigate their new lives in America.

Compensation for losses showed perhaps the starkest disparity. The White Star Line's settlements followed a clear hierarchy:

- First-class claims were typically settled quickly and generously
- Second-class passengers received moderate compensation after more extended negotiations
- Steerage passengers often got minimal settlements, if any
- Crew members' families had to fight for even basic compensation

Some survivors channeled their trauma into advocacy. Second-class passenger Charlotte Collyer, who survived with her eight-year-old daughter but lost her husband, became an outspoken critic of maritime safety regulations. Despite financial struggles and working as a waitress to support her daughter, she continued to give interviews and write articles advocating for reform.[2]

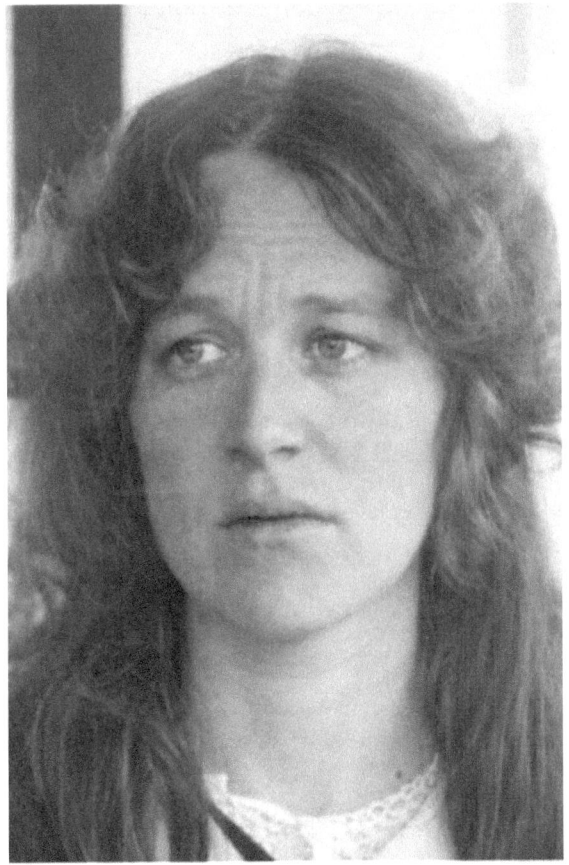

Charlotte Colyer

Titanic's third class included a wide array of emigrants whose experiences further underscore how uneven survival was across nationality, gender, and circumstance. Many came from Central and Eastern Europe, often recorded not by modern nation-states but under the umbrella of the Austro-Hungarian Empire.

Among these were at least 37 Croatian passengers, of whom only three survived—one of the lowest survival rates of any identifiable national group on board. Other passengers from the empire—Slovak, Slovenian, Hungarian, and related backgrounds—were present in notable numbers, and survival among them was rare, particularly for adult males traveling alone.[3]

Smaller groups from Western and Southern Europe were also part of the steerage population. Four Portuguese passengers boarded Titanic; none survived. French, Belgian, Italian, German, and Swiss emigrants were likewise present, often as individuals or small family units rather than large clusters. Their numbers were comparatively modest, and survival statistics vary by source. Still, as with most third-class groups, outcomes followed the same grim pattern: women and children fared better than men, and those traveling alone were especially vulnerable.

One third-class group stands out for a different reason. Eight Chinese men boarded Titanic, and six survived—an unusually high survival rate given both their class and gender. Their escape, long obscured and later complicated by racialized reporting and deportation upon arrival, has since been carefully reconstructed by modern historians.

Taken together, these disparate national experiences reveal that Titanic's loss was not evenly distributed. Survival was shaped not only by chance but also by language, mobility, timing, and proximity—both physical and social—to the means of escape when the ship's final hour arrived.

Lebanese Passengers on Titanic

There were just over 100 Lebanese aboard Titanic, mainly in third class, many traveling as families or as young women bound for relatives in the United States. When the ship sank, only thirty survived. The pattern was stark and familiar: women and children escaped in disproportionate numbers, while very few men did.

For this community, the disaster was not only a maritime tragedy but a rupture that erased entire family lines in a single night.

The survivors' stories reflect both vulnerability and resolve. Women such as Shaanineh Abi-Saab endured the chaos of evacuation and the uncertainty that followed, often arriving in America alone or to news of devastating loss. The Baclini sisters, who survived together, became emblematic of the fragile threads of family that held through the catastrophe. Their survival did not soften the blow; it sharpened it, carrying the memory of those who did not make it forward.

Others were remembered not for survival, but for how they faced death. Moubarak Assi was recalled in later accounts as having danced as the end approached—a gesture interpreted by witnesses as defiance, despair, or an attempt to steady those around him. Whether literal or embellished, such stories reveal how Lebanese passengers were seen and remembered: not as anonymous steerage statistics, but as individuals responding to catastrophe with fear, courage, and humanity.[4]

Tu'mah Family

When Hinnah Tu'mah and her children finally reached New York, they were taken first to St. Vincent's Hospital to recover, then continued to Dowagiac, Michigan, where her husband, Darwīsh Tu'mah, was living.

He knew his family had set out for America, but not that they were sailing aboard Titanic. The news reached him only after the disaster, when a telegram arrived from his wife. They had survived. The words carried both relief and shock, a confirmation of life delivered through the narrowest margin of chance.

In Dowagiac, the family began to put down roots and gradually anglicized their names; Darwīsh became Thomas, and Hinnah became Anna. Over the next few years, they welcomed three more children—Sam (1913–1997), Francis (1914–1965), and Joseph (1916–1995)—before relocating to Flint, Michigan, where their son Jirjis, now known as George, ran a grocery store.[5]

Anna was widowed in June 1946 when Thomas died, and she later went to live in Los Angeles with her three youngest sons, returning to Michigan in the summers to visit the rest of the family.

Her youngest son, Joe, became a doctor in North Hollywood. He had served in the U.S. Army during the Second World War and later in Korea, where he was assigned to a MASH unit.

Anna eventually returned to Michigan, settling into a life shaped less by loss than by continuity. Surrounded by a widening circle of grandchildren and great-grandchildren, she was remembered as a gentle presence, her speech a soft weave of English and Arabic that carried echoes of the world she had crossed and the one she had made her own.

She died at Genesee Memorial Hospital on 28 June 1976, aged 91. Decades later, in 2008, her grandson Joseph Thomas (Jirjis/George's son) published a family memoir, *Grandma Survived the Titanic*, recounting their escape from the ship and the life they built afterward; he himself died that August in Genesee, Michigan.

Swedish Survivors

Swedish emigrants suffered terrible losses, especially those in Third Class. With about 100 Swedish passengers aboard and only 34 surviving, roughly two-thirds of them died as the ship went down. Most were third-class travelers heading to new lives in America, and being deep in the ship, far from the lifeboats, they found escape far more difficult.

Behind those numbers were shattered families. The Anderssons—Anders, his wife Alfrida, and their five young children—were all lost; only a family portrait remained to tell their story.

Other families were also shattered: The Asplund family was torn in two when father Carl and three sons died, while mother Selma and children Lillian and Felix managed to reach a boat and survive. Alma Pålsson and her children also perished, leaving her husband Nils to carry on alone, overwhelmed by grief. Edvard Lindell survived on Collapsible A, but his wife Gerda died in the icy water nearby, a moment other survivors would never forget.[6]

A few Swedish families and individuals did find safety. Agnes Sandström and her daughters, Marguerite and Beatrice, were among the few third-class families rescued, taken aboard Lifeboat 13. In that same boat was Anna Sofia Nysten, one of the fortunate few whose journey to America continued.

Anna Sophia Nysten remained in New York until 1915, carefully setting aside money for a long-imagined return to Sweden and a reunion with the family she had left behind. Then came the sinking of Lusitania. The disaster rippled far beyond the North Atlantic, reaching her in New York and unsettling plans that suddenly felt fragile. Faced with the reminder of how easily the sea could undo even the most carefully laid intentions, she hesitated — and began to reconsider the journey home.

That year, she moved to Iowa, settling in Des Moines, where she married fellow Swede Frans Otto Arvid Gustafsson in 1920. She returned to Sweden several times during her lifetime and had many grandchildren in her later years. Following a week-long illness, Anna died on March 28, 1977, from surgical complications.

For the Swedish community, Titanic became a symbol of broken hopes: entire family lines ended in one night, and dreams of a better life were swallowed by the Atlantic, underscoring how dangerous and unequal the situation was for those in third class.

Grupp af några af de å Sv. luth. Emigranthemmet inkvarterade räddade svenskarna. — I bakgrunden hemmets föreståndare, pastor Lillia.

A group of rescued Swedes was accommodated at the Swedish Lutheran Emigrant Home.

Irish Passengers

For Ireland, Titanic was not a distant headline—it was personal. Queenstown (today Cobh) was the last port, and from it came a concentrated group of third-class emigrants—young women, married couples, friends traveling in clusters—carrying letters, savings, and the fragile certainty that America would be better than what they were leaving. When the ship went down, the numbers told a harsh story: among the 113 Irish third-class emigrants identified by the British Inquiry, only 40 lived, and the survivors were overwhelmingly women. Just seven men made it out.[7]

That imbalance shaped how the loss was felt back home. Communities did not just mourn individuals; they mourned futures—husbands lost, brothers gone, wage-earners who had been expected to send money home or build the first foothold for relatives to follow.

In places like rural Mayo, the catastrophe became a local wound measured in empty chairs and lost dreams. At the same time, the survivors carried a different burden: they had reached the lifeboats but returned to a world that now asked them to explain why they lived when so many of their men did not.

Daniel Buckley

Now safely settled in Manhattan, Daniel was one of the few third-class passengers called to testify at the American Inquiry into the sinking.

He wrote and published a poem shortly after the disaster.[8]

Saturday, 1 June 1912
By Dannie Buckley of Kingwilliamstown, Co. Cork, a Survivor
of the Wreck
Sincerest sympathy goes out today
From every heart to friends of those
who sleep.
From kindred and dear homeland
far away,
Within the deep.
And in a special manner for our isle,
When we think of our own beloved

beloved dead.
The toilers of the sea, who perished
while
in quest of bread.
Some sailed expecting to clasp lovingly
Their own beyond the waves, and
others sighed,
For leaving souls they ne'er again
might see
Where mortals bide.

Daniel was paid $1,000 for relief assistance after the disaster. He stayed in Manhattan, working at a hotel until 1917, when he enlisted in the army for World War I.

Daniel arrived in France in the fall of 1917 with Company K of the 165th U.S. Infantry. On October 15, 1918, Buckley was killed by a sniper while helping to retrieve wounded soldiers on the Meuse-Argonne front. He was initially buried in France, but his remains were taken to Ireland in the spring of 1919.

The Crew

Nearly 900 crew members sailed aboard Titanic, with only 214 surviving.

Many of those who did not survive were working below decks—firemen, trimmers, engineers—men whose labor kept the ship functioning long enough for others to escape. These figures do not describe heroism or failure on an individual level. They describe structure.

They reflect who was closest to the lifeboats, who received information first, who was expected to wait, and who was required to keep working. They show how survival followed lines already drawn long before the ship struck ice. When the sea finally took Titanic, it did not choose at random. It followed the map the ship had already made.

Reginald Robinson Lee

Titanic's lookout on the fateful night, Reginald Lee, also testified in inquiries after the disaster:

"Three bells were struck by Fleet, warning "Right ahead," and immediately he rung the telephone up to the bridge, "Iceberg right ahead." The reply came back from the bridge, "Thank you."

Within the year, he returned to Southampton and continued a career at sea. He was found dead on August 6, 1913, from heart failure following pneumonia and pleurisy. He was 43.

Frederick Barrett

After Titanic, Frederick Barrett testified at both the British Wreck Commissioner's inquiry and the United States Senate inquiry into the sinking of the Titanic. He returned to sea within weeks of the sinking, joining Titanic's sister ship, RMS Olympic.

He stayed on as a fireman at sea for over a decade, then moved to work as a timberman. At the age of 48, in 1931, he died from pulmonary tuberculosis.

Family of Joseph Bell

Joseph Bell left behind a wife and four children whose lives were altered not by a single dramatic moment but by a permanent absence. There would be no body returned, no grave to visit—only a name on a list and the knowledge that he had remained at his post as time ran out.

For families like Bell's, the aftermath was not heroic or cinematic. It was practical and relentless. A lost income meant immediate uncertainty: how to pay rent, how to feed children, how to plan a future that had once assumed a working husband and father. Widows were expected to endure quietly, and children to grow up quickly. The world moved on, but the loss did not. In the years that followed, Joseph's sacrifice lived on not in monuments or headlines, but in the daily resilience of a family forced to rebuild around a space that could never be filled.

As decades passed, the survivors aged, and their numbers dwindled. Each carried their own version of that night, their memories shaped by class, circumstance, and the long echo of trauma. The last Titanic survivor, Millvina Dean, died in 2009 at age 97, marking the end of living memory of the disaster.

Yet the impact of Titanic continues to ripple through families, maritime law, and our understanding of how disaster affects people across social boundaries.

[1] "Sarah Roth," Encyclopedia Titanica.

[2] "Charlotte Annie Collyer," Encyclopedia Titanica.

[3] Steven Schwankert, The Six: The Untold Story of the Titanic's Chinese Survivors (London: Pegasus Books, 2025).

[4] "The Lebanese on the Titanic: Dancing at the Edge of Tragedy," The Beirutier.

[5] Titanic Recollections," South Bend Tribune, February 13, 1998.

[6] William Robbins, "Screams, Then Sea's Silence, Still Haunt 5 Survivors of Titanic," New York Times, April 18, 1982.

[7] British Board of Trade, Report into the Loss of the RMS Titanic (1912).

[8] Daniel Buckley, "The Titanic Disaster," The Advocate, June 1, 1912.

Closing Thoughts

The sinking of Titanic is remembered for its grandeur and horror, but the lives beneath those labels—engineers who stayed at their posts, immigrant women who shepherded children, laborers whose names vanished with their wages—reveal what the disaster actually was: a collision between modern systems and human vulnerability. Stripped of sentiment, the record shows who was visible, who was protected, and who was expected to absorb risk without recognition.

Again and again, the evidence points to labor's invisibility. Crew members such as engineers, firemen, stewards, and wireless operators were essential to the ship's operation yet largely absent from its mythology. When the emergency came, their work did not stop; it intensified even as escape narrowed. Their deaths were not accidents of fate but consequences of duty embedded in the hierarchy. The ship survived as long as it did because of them, yet history remembered them last.

The disaster also exposes how class shaped survival. Access to information, proximity to lifeboats, clarity of instruction, and even physical pathways through the ship were not evenly distributed. Class was not merely a social distinction—it was a logistical one, written into steel corridors and locked gates. When systems failed, those divisions did not dissolve; they hardened. The sea was indifferent, but the ship was not.

These patterns are not relics of 1912. Modern disasters—industrial accidents, environmental crises, pandemics—continue to reveal the same fault lines: essential workers bearing disproportionate risk, marginalized communities suffering the heaviest losses, and accountability diffused after the fact.

Titanic endures not because it was unique, but because it was early. Its legacy is a warning: technology does not erase inequality, and progress without responsibility only shifts who pays the price.

Titanic was not undone by a single moment of arrogance or a single failure of vigilance. It was undone by a system that normalized risk, relied on labor to absorb danger, and treated problems as manageable until they were no longer so.

Acknowledgements

This book rests on the work of countless historians, archivists, librarians, and researchers who have spent more than a century preserving the records of Titanic — often fragmentary, sometimes contradictory, always human. Passenger lists, inquiry transcripts, letters, affidavits, newspapers, and family histories made it possible to move beyond legend and return names, context, and consequence to those too often reduced to statistics.

I am especially indebted to the modern scholars and independent researchers who continue to question inherited narratives, challenge class-blind retellings, and recover overlooked communities—immigrants, crew, laborers, and families whose experiences shaped the disaster but rarely shaped its mythology. Their insistence on evidence over romance has guided the tone and structure of this work.

Finally, this book owes a quiet debt to the passengers and crew themselves. Many left little behind beyond a name, a testimony, or a single remembered act. To treat those fragments with care—to resist embellishment while honoring meaning—has been the central obligation of this project. Any errors remain my own.

Notes on Sources

This book draws on a layered historical record: official investigations, contemporary reporting, ship documentation, survivor testimony, and later scholarship that re-examines the evidence with the benefit of distance and additional sources. Where accounts conflict—as they often do in Titanic history—I prioritize contemporaneous documents and clearly attributable statements over later retellings. Widely repeated details that lack firm sourcing are either omitted or identified as uncertain.

The foundation of the factual narrative comes from the two official post-disaster investigations: the United States Senate Inquiry (1912) and the British Wreck Commissioner's Inquiry (the "Mersey Report," 1912). These records preserve sworn testimony, timelines, and operational details—ice warnings, speed, lifeboat handling, wireless practices, and crew procedure—and remain essential for understanding both what happened and how responsibility was assessed in the immediate aftermath.

Where available, I also rely on ship and company documentation such as passenger and crew lists, deck plans, technical specifications, and wireless logs or summaries of wireless traffic. For individual lives, I draw on letters, postcards, affidavits, and family documents when these materials can be traced to an archive or to reputable historical publications.

Newspapers from April through June 1912 provide immediacy: names, early survivor interviews, public reaction, and the evolving first accounts of the disaster. Because early reporting was often rushed and occasionally inaccurate, newspaper claims are used primarily to capture contemporary language and perception, and are cross-checked against inquiry testimony or later vetted scholarship before being treated as factual.

For passenger biographies, demographics, and cross-referenced survival outcomes, I rely on established reference works and curated research databases maintained by long-standing Titanic historians and institutions. These resources are especially useful for aggregation—nationality, port of embarkation, family groupings, and post-disaster lives—though categories such as "nationality" can vary in meaning and are clarified in the text when relevant.

Descriptions of daily life aboard the ship—third-class spaces, meal service, movement between decks, and steerage conditions—are based on ship plans, company practices on contemporary liners, and survivor accounts. When reconstructing routine experience, I rely on well-documented patterns rather than inventing specific actions or dialogue.

Some of the most memorable Titanic stories are also the least reliable. Anecdotal material is included only when it can be traced to a named witness, a published memoir or interview with clear provenance, or a respected historical work that cites underlying documentation. When a story is widely reported but not verifiable, it is treated as reported tradition rather than established fact.

Citations are provided so readers can follow the evidence if they wish. Those using this book as a starting point for further research will find the inquiry transcripts and contemporary documentation the most direct sources, while modern works are most useful for context, cross-checking, and locating scattered primary material.

About the Author

Alina Rush is neither a Titanic specialist nor a maritime historian. Like countless others, her interest in the ship and its sinking grew from a lifelong fascination—one shaped by memory, repetition, and the unanswered questions that cling to the disaster more than a century later. What drew her to this project was not the mythology of Titanic but the people who lived and worked within it and the way so many of their stories have faded beneath familiar headlines.

Rush brings more than twenty-five years of experience crafting narratives for marginalized communities worldwide. Her work has focused on restoring context, dignity, and voice to lives often reduced to footnotes or stereotypes.

She is also the daughter of immigrants who made their own harrowing journeys to America aboard ocean liners like Titanic in the early twentieth century. This book is written in recognition that migration, labor, and loss were not abstractions—they were lived realities carried across the Atlantic by ordinary people whose hopes were larger than the ships that carried them.

A Note from the Author

If this book helped you see Titanic differently—less as a legend, more as a lived experience—I would be grateful if you shared your experience by leaving a review. Reviews matter not as praise, but as signals to other readers that these stories are worth encountering. Even a brief, honest review helps keep books like this visible.

This title is part of a larger body of work published by Unbound Press, dedicated to overlooked histories, marginalized voices, and rigorously researched nonfiction. If this approach resonates with you, I invite you to explore the full catalog. Each book asks a similar question: whose stories were carried forward, and whose were left behind?

More titles like this are available at www.UnboundPressBooks.com.

Thank you for reading—and for helping these histories continue to be read.

Appendix

Lifeboats: Lifeboat Tally

Boat 1 — 12 aboard

Boat 2 — 18 aboard

Boat 3 — 32 aboard

Boat 4 — 30 aboard

Boat 5 — 36 aboard

Boat 6 — 24 aboard

Boat 7 — 28 aboard

Boat 8 — 27 aboard

Boat 9 — 40 aboard

Boat 10 — 57 aboard

Boat 11 — 50 aboard

Boat 12 — 41 aboard

Boat 13 — 55 aboard

Boat 14 — 40 aboard

Boat 15 — 66 aboard

Boat 16 — 52 aboard

Boat A — 13 aboard

Boat B — 28 aboard

Boat C — 43 aboard

Boat D — 20 aboard

Total persons saved by lifeboats: 712
Emergency Lifeboat 1 (Starboard)

Launch time: Approximately 1:10 a.m.

Officer(s) in charge: First Officer William Murdoch; Fifth Officer Harold Lowe; Lookout George Symons (placed in command)

Rated capacity: 40 persons

Estimated number aboard at launch: 12

Emergency Lifeboat 1 was the first of Titanic's two emergency cutters to be launched with only 12 aboard: seven crew members and five First Class passengers.

The composition of the boat reflected Murdoch's discretionary interpretation of "women and children first," under which married couples and individual men had already been permitted to board other lifeboats. Several first-class male passengers were allowed to board with Murdoch's consent. Murdoch also directed several crewmen to enter the boat and placed Lookout George Symons in command.

After the Titanic sank, the boat did not return to attempt water rescues. Later testimony conflicted as to whether such a return was proposed or discussed among those aboard.

RMS Carpathia recovered Emergency Lifeboat 1.

Selected occupants:
– George Symons, Lookout (in command)
– Sir Cosmo Duff-Gordon and his wife, Lucy
– Laura Mabel Francatelli

Emergency Lifeboat 2 (Port)

Launch time: Approximately 1:45 a.m.

Officer(s) in charge: Captain Edward J. Smith; Chief Officer
Henry Wilde; Fourth Officer Joseph Groves Boxhall
(placed in command)

Rated capacity: 40 persons

Estimated number aboard at launch: Approximately 18

Emergency Lifeboat 2, the second of Titanic's two cutters,
departed carrying only about 18 persons, primarily
women, along with one male third-class passenger who
boarded to accompany his wife and young child.

After Titanic sank, Fourth Officer Boxhall proposed
returning to rescue people in the water, but the occupants
refused.

At approximately 4:00 a.m., Boxhall sighted RMS
Carpathia on the horizon and fired a green flare to signal
the ship. Emergency Lifeboat 2 became the first lifeboat to
reach Carpathia, arriving at approximately 4:10 a.m.

RMS Carpathia recovered Emergency Lifeboat 2 at
approximately 4:10 a.m.

Selected occupants:

– Joseph Groves Boxhall, Fourth Officer (in command)
– Anton Kink, with his wife Louise and daughter
– Charlotte Appleton
– Mallvina Cornell
– Minnie Coutts and her sons William and Neville

Lifeboat 3 (Starboard)

Launch time: Approximately 1:00 a.m.

Officer(s) in charge: First Officer William Murdoch; Fifth Officer Harold Lowe; Able Seaman George Moore (placed in command)

Rated capacity: 65 persons

Estimated number aboard at launch: Approximately 32

As with earlier launches, many passengers did not fully grasp the seriousness of the situation. Railroad executive Charles Melville Hays escorted his wife, daughter, and maid into the boat but did not attempt to board. Contemporary accounts describe the embarkation at this time as calm and orderly, with little outward panic.

Survivors described the atmosphere on deck during the launch as formal and almost unreal. The ship's band continued to play, and passengers reportedly laughed and conversed as the boats were lowered.

Lifeboat 3 was rescued by RMS Carpathia at approximately 7:30 a.m.

Selected occupants:

– George Moore, Able Seaman (in command)
– Myra and Henry S. Harper, and their Pekinese dog Sun
Yat Sen
– Charlotte Wardle Cardeza and her son Thomas
– Frederic and Margaretta Spedden with their son Robert
– Albert and Vera Dick

Lifeboat 4 (Port)

Launch time: Approximately 1:50 a.m.

Officer(s) in charge: Second Officer Charles Lightoller;
Quartermaster Walter Perkis (placed in command)

Rated capacity: 65 persons

Estimated number aboard at launch: Approximately 34

Lifeboat 4 was the last of the wooden lifeboats to be
lowered. To allow boarding, windows in the Promenade
enclosure were forced open, and deck chairs were stacked
to form makeshift steps. While men were generally
excluded, one adolescent boy was permitted to enter after
his father intervened. After launch, Perkis maneuvered the
boat along the ship's side to search for additional
passengers at open gangways but found none.

Shortly after Titanic sank, Lifeboat 4 immediately returned
to the wreck site, making it the only lifeboat to do so
without delay. It recovered several men from the water,
though two later died from exposure.

Lifeboat 4 later received additional survivors transferred from Lifeboat 14 and Collapsible Boat D. By daylight, the boat was heavily occupied but remained seaworthy.

Lifeboat 4 reached RMS Carpathia at approximately 8:00.

Selected occupants:

– Madeleine Talmage Astor, with her maid and nurse
– Emily Borie Ryerson and her children
– Lucile Polk Carter and her children

Lifeboat 5 (Starboard)

Launch time: Approximately 12:55 a.m.

Officer(s) in charge: First Officer William Murdoch; Third Officer Herbert Pitman (placed in command)

Rated capacity: 65 persons

Estimated number aboard at launch: Approximately 36

Primarily launched with women and children, but at a time when many passengers remained unconvinced of the seriousness of the situation. Several declined to board. White Star Line chairman J. Bruce Ismay actively urged Pitman to begin loading women and children and assisted in directing passengers into the boat.

The lowering of Lifeboat 5 was slow and difficult. Newly painted pulleys and stiff ropes caused the boat to descend unevenly and in jerks. Following Titanic's sinking, several occupants were transferred to Lifeboat 7. Pitman proposed returning to the wreck site for rescue but abandoned the attempt after protests from passengers who feared the risk. The decision weighed on Pitman for the rest of his life.

RMS Carpathia rescued lifeboat 5 at approximately 6:00 a.m.

Selected occupants:

– Herbert Pitman, Third Officer
– Ruth Dodge and her son Washington Dodge Jr. (the first child placed in a lifeboat)
– Henry and Clara Frauenthal
– Karl Behr and members of the Beckwith family

Lifeboat 6 (Port)

Launch time: Approximately 12:55 a.m.

Officer(s) in charge: Captain Edward J. Smith; Second Officer Charles Lightoller; Quartermaster Robert Hichens (placed in command)

Rated capacity: 65 persons

Estimated number aboard at launch: Approximately 24

Lifeboat 6 was launched significantly under capacity. Margaret "Molly" Brown did not board voluntarily but was physically placed into the boat by a crewman as it was being lowered.

During lowering, concerns about insufficient manpower led Lightoller to request assistance from experienced personnel on deck. Major Arthur Godfrey Peuchen volunteered and descended into the boat, becoming the only adult male passenger permitted by Lightoller to board a lifeboat.

Relations aboard Lifeboat 6 were strained. Hichens and Peuchen clashed over authority and rowing duties. After Titanic sank, repeated appeals to return to rescue people in the water were rejected by Hichens. He also resisted efforts by female passengers to assist with rowing to keep warm. Despite his objections, Margaret Brown organized the women into rowing shifts, with support from other passengers.

Lifeboat 6 later tied up with Lifeboat 16 and remained at sea for several hours. One passenger, Mrs. Elizabeth Rothschild, brought a Pomeranian aboard, one of the few dogs to survive the disaster.

Lifeboat 6 was among the last boats to reach RMS Carpathia, coming alongside at approximately 8:00 a.m.

Selected occupants:
– Robert Hichens, Quartermaster (in command)
– Frederick Fleet, Lookout
– Margaret Brown
– Helen Churchill Candee
– Arthur Godfrey Peuchen

Lifeboat 6 rowing towards RMS Carpathia on April 15, 1912

Lifeboat 7 (Starboard)

Launch time: Approximately 12:45 a.m.

Officer(s) in charge: First Officer William Murdoch; Fifth Officer Harold Lowe

Rated capacity: 65 persons

Estimated number aboard at launch: Approximately 28

Lifeboat 7 was the first lifeboat launched. Testimony given later indicated that officers were concerned about the structural integrity of the lifeboats if lowered fully loaded and intended to add people once they reached the water.

Lifeboat 7 was launched without its drain plug in place, causing water to enter the boat. The leak was temporarily controlled using clothing, but the occupants sat with their feet in freezing water. After Titanic sank at 2:20 a.m., those aboard heard the cries of people in the water. The occupants rejected a suggestion to return and render assistance.

The lifeboat drifted for some time before coming alongside Lifeboat 5. Several passengers were transferred from Lifeboat 5 into Lifeboat 7 due to overcrowding, after which the two boats were lashed together for the remainder of the night. Lifeboat 7 separated from Lifeboat 5 in daylight and was later recovered by RMS Carpathia.

Selected occupants:
– Dorothy Gibson, actress
– Margaret Hays
– Archie Jewell, lookout
– Alfred Nourney

Lifeboat 8 (Port)

Launch time: Approximately 1:10 a.m.

Officer(s) in charge: Captain Edward J. Smith; Chief Officer Henry Wilde; Able Seaman Thomas William Jones (placed in command)

Rated capacity: 65 persons

Estimated number aboard at launch: Approximately 27

Lifeboat 8 was the first lifeboat lowered on the port side. During loading, Isidor and Ida Straus were offered places, but both refused. They were last seen together on deck.

Major Archibald Butt escorted a female passenger to the boat and assisted others before remaining aboard. Following the sinking, Jones proposed returning for rescue, but the majority objected, fearing the boat would be swamped. One passenger, Noëlle, Countess of Rothes, took an active role in managing the boat, assisting with steering, rowing, and organizing occupants. They spent several hours rowing toward lights believed to be another ship. At daylight, the boat reversed course when RMS Carpathia was sighted approaching from the opposite direction.

Lifeboat 8 was recovered at approximately 7:30 a.m. Selected occupants:
– Noëlle, Countess of Rothes
– Marie Grice Young
– Ella Holmes White

Lifeboat 9 (Starboard)

Launch time: Approximately 1:20 a.m.

Officer(s) in charge: First Officer William Murdoch; Sixth Officer James Moody; Purser Hugh McElroy; Boatswain's Mate Albert Hames (placed in command)

Rated capacity: 65 persons

Estimated number aboard at launch: Approximately 40

Lifeboat 9 was launched with primarily women, and a small number of men were admitted only after no other women came forward. Several passengers initially resisted boarding. One elderly woman refused outright and returned below decks. May Futrelle was also reluctant to leave until urged strongly by her husband, novelist Jacques Futrelle, who remained behind and later perished. Benjamin Guggenheim escorted his companion and her maid into Lifeboat 9 before retiring to his stateroom. Other male passengers were prevented from boarding despite appeals from women already in the boat.

Lifeboat 9 remained clear of the wreck site and did not attempt a return, and was recovered at approximately 6:15.

Selected occupants:
– May Futrelle
– Léontine Aubart
– Kate Buss

Lifeboat 10 (Port)

Launch time: Approximately 1:47 a.m.

Officer(s) in charge: Chief Officer Henry Wilde; First Officer William Murdoch; Able Seaman Edward Buley (placed in command)

Rated capacity: 65 persons

Estimated number aboard at launch: Approximately 57

Lifeboat 10 was launched when Titanic was listing heavily to port, creating a widening gap between the deck and the lifeboats and making boarding increasingly hazardous. As urgency increased, loading became rapid and chaotic.

Several passengers boarded with difficulty, including one woman who narrowly avoided falling between the ship and the boat. Children were rushed aboard, and at least one infant was passed directly into the lifeboat. A third-class passenger jumped into the boat as it was being lowered.

Lifeboat 10 was the second-to-last lifeboat recovered by RMS Carpathia, coming alongside at approximately 8:00 a.m.

Selected occupants:

– Edward Buley, Able Seaman (in command)

– Millvina Dean, with her mother and brother

– Masabumi Hosono

– Barbara West and her family

Lifeboat 11 (Starboard)

Launch time: Approximately 1:37 a.m.

Officer(s) in charge: First Officer William Murdoch; Able Seaman Sidney Humphreys (placed in command)

Rated capacity: 65 persons

Estimated number aboard at launch: Approximately 70

Lifeboat 11 departed heavily loaded, carrying an estimated 70 persons aboard, exceeding its rated capacity. During loading, one steward was knocked into the boat while assisting passengers, reflecting the increasingly crowded and urgent conditions on deck. A Second Class mother was initially prevented from boarding after her children were placed aboard, but ultimately succeeded in entering. However, one of her daughters was left behind and directed to another lifeboat. Upon reaching the water, Lifeboat 11 was nearly swamped by a powerful stream of water being discharged from the ship in an attempt to control flooding. Passengers were tightly packed, and some were forced to stand as the boat pulled away.

Lifeboat 11 was recovered by RMS Carpathia at approximately 7:00 a.m.

Selected occupants:

– Sidney Humphreys, Able Seaman (in command)
– Edith Louise Rosenbaum
– Alice Catherine Cooper
– Annie Robinson, stewardess
– Jane Quick and her daughters May and Winnifred

Lifeboat 12 (Port)

Launch time: Approximately 1:35 a.m.

Officer(s) in charge: Chief Officer Henry Wilde; Second Officer Charles Lightoller; Able Seaman John Poingdestre (placed in command)

Rated capacity: 65 persons

Estimated number aboard at launch: Approximately 28–30

Lifeboat 12 was lowered with primarily second-class passengers and crew.

After Titanic sank, Lifeboat 12 became heavily involved in redistribution and rescue operations, coordinating with Lifeboats 4, 10, 14, and Collapsible D. Later, Lifeboat 12—together with Lifeboat 4—responded to Second Officer Lightoller's whistle from the overturned Collapsible B. The boat rescued approximately 16 survivors standing on the upturned hull. Command of Lifeboat 12 subsequently passed to Lightoller.

By the end of these transfers and rescue efforts, Lifeboat 12 was heavily overloaded, carrying an estimated 60 to 70 persons, well beyond its intended capacity. Despite this, the boat remained afloat and operational.

Lifeboat 12 was the last lifeboat recovered by RMS Carpathia, coming alongside at approximately 8:30 a.m.

Selected occupants:
– John Poingdestre, Able Seaman (initially in command)
– Charles Lightoller, Second Officer (later in command)
– Frederick Clench, Able Seaman

Lifeboat 13 (Starboard)

Launch time: Approximately 1:43 a.m.

Officer(s) in charge: First Officer William Murdoch; Sixth Officer James Moody; Leading Fireman Frederick William Barrett (placed in command)

Rated capacity: 65 persons

Estimated number aboard at launch: Approximately 70

Lifeboat 13 was launched heavily occupied, carrying an estimated 70 persons aboard. The majority of passengers were women and children from Second and Third Class.

While being lowered, Lifeboat 13 was nearly swamped by a powerful stream of water being expelled from the ship's condenser exhaust. Occupants were forced to fend the boat off using oars and spars. The wash from the exhaust caused the boat to drift directly beneath Lifeboat 15, which was descending at the same time. Lifeboat 15's lowering was halted just in time to avoid crushing Lifeboat 13. The falls of Lifeboat 13 jammed and had to be cut free before the boat could clear the ship.

Lifeboat 13 was recovered by RMS Carpathia at approximately 6:30 a.m.

Selected occupants:

– Frederick William Barrett, Leading Fireman (in command)
– Lawrence Beesley
– Reginald Robinson Lee, Lookout
– Frederick Dent Ray

Lifeboat 14 (Port)

Launch time: Approximately 1:30 a.m.

Officer(s) in charge: Chief Officer Henry Wilde; Second Officer Charles Lightoller; Fifth Officer Harold Godfrey Lowe; Sixth Officer James Moody; Harold Godfrey Lowe (placed in command)

Rated capacity: 65 persons

Estimated number aboard at launch: Approximately 40

Lifeboat 14 launched as Titanic was already listing noticeably. After Titanic sank, Lowe gathered several nearby boats—Lifeboats 4, 10, 12, and Collapsible D—and redistributed passengers to reduce overcrowding. He then assembled a volunteer crew and returned Lifeboat 14 to the wreck site in an attempt to rescue survivors from the water.

Lifeboat 14 was one of only two boats to return for rescue. Four men were pulled from the sea; one later died, while three survived. Several hours later, the survivors from Collapsible Boat A, which was near sinking, were brought aboard Lifeboat 14. Lowe also rigged a mast and sail to improve speed and maneuverability, making Lifeboat 14 the only lifeboat to employ sail power during the rescue efforts.

Lifeboat 14 reached RMS Carpathia at approximately 7:15.

Selected occupants:
– Eva Hart and her mother Esther Hart
– Edith Eileen Brown and her mother Elizabeth
– Marjorie Collyer and her mother Charlotte

Lifeboat 15 (Starboard)

Launch time: Approximately 1:45 a.m.

Officer(s) in charge: First Officer William Murdoch; Sixth Officer James Moody; Fireman Frank Dymond (placed in command)

Rated capacity: 65 persons

Estimated number aboard at launch: Approximately 70

Lifeboat 15 was lowered almost simultaneously with Lifeboat 13, and departed heavily loaded, with an estimated 70 persons aboard, making it one of the most crowded boats launched from Titanic.

The boat sat extremely low in the water at launch, with later testimony describing the gunwales as nearly awash.

Due to the heavy load, conditions aboard were cramped and precarious. Passengers reported that even slight movement caused the boat to dip close to the waterline. Despite this, Lifeboat 15 cleared the ship safely and remained afloat throughout the night.

Lifeboat 15 was among the last boats recovered by RMS Carpathia, coming alongside at approximately 7:30 a.m.

Selected occupants:

– Frank Dymond, Fireman (in command)
– Lillian Asplund, with her mother Selma and brother Felix

- Arthur John Priest, Fireman
- Alfred Frank Evans, Lookout
- George Cavell, Trimmer

Lifeboat 16 (Port)

Launch time: Approximately 1:25 a.m.

Officer(s) in charge: Chief Officer Henry Wilde; Sixth Officer James Moody; Master-at-Arms Joseph Henry Bailey (placed in command)

Rated capacity: 65 persons

Estimated number aboard at launch: Approximately 53

Lifeboat 16 was launched with a comparatively large number of passengers, most of whom were women and children from Second and Third Class. At one point, it encountered Lifeboat 6 and transferred a fireman to assist with rowing.

Accounts from Third Class passengers describe the embarkation as orderly and calm, with little sense of panic. The ship remained fully illuminated, and music continued to play as the lifeboats were launched. Passengers later recalled witnessing Titanic's final breakup and the cries from the water that followed, followed by an abrupt silence. Survivors later described profound shock and emotional distress following rescue, with many passengers struggling to process what they had witnessed during the night.

Selected occupants:

– – Violet Constance Jessop, stewardess

– Evelyn Marsden, stewardess

– Elizabeth Leather, stewardess

– Margaret Mannion

Collapsible Lifeboat A (Starboard)

Launch time: Not successfully launched; washed off the deck during the final plunge.

Officer(s) in charge: Chief Officer Henry Wilde; First Officer William Murdoch; Sixth Officer James Moody

Rated capacity: 47 persons

Estimated number aboard: Unknown at separation; approximately 14 survivors remained alive

Collapsible Lifeboat A was brought onto the Boat Deck upright at approximately 2:05 a.m. and was in the process of being launched when Titanic's final plunge caused the lifeboat to be washed off the deck at approximately 2:15 a.m. In the ensuing chaos, the boat drifted away from the ship, partially submerged, with water flooding the interior. Several passengers entered the boat directly from the sea. Many occupants succumbed to hypothermia or fell back into the water during the night. By morning, only about 14 people remained alive aboard Collapsible A.

Survivors from Collapsible Lifeboat A were rescued by Lifeboat 14 during a return to the wreck site. Some survivors were later transferred to Collapsible Lifeboat D. Survivors were taken aboard RMS Carpathia via other lifeboats. Collapsible Lifeboat A itself was later recovered approximately one month after the disaster with several bodies still aboard.

Selected occupants:

– Rhoda Mary Abbott

– Olaus Abelseth

Collapsible Lifeboat B (Port)

Launch time: Not launched; washed off the deck during the final plunge.

Officer(s) in charge: Second Officer Charles Lightoller (assumed command after capsizing)

Rated capacity: 47 persons

Estimated number aboard: Approximately 30–35 initially on hull; about 28 survived until transfer

At approximately 2:10 a.m., Second Officer Lightoller attempted to free the boat from the roof of the officers' quarters. During the attempt, the lifeboat broke through the ramp and landed upside down on the Boat Deck. There was no opportunity to right it before Titanic entered its final plunge.

At approximately 2:15 a.m., water swept across the Boat Deck, washing the overturned lifeboat and numerous people into the sea.

As the ship sank, the forward funnel collapsed into the water, forcing Collapsible B farther from the wreck. Several dozen men managed to climb onto the overturned hull, including Lightoller, as well as senior crew members and first-class passengers. Wireless operator Harold Bride escaped from beneath the hull after being temporarily trapped in an air pocket.

The boat floated keel-up, supported by a diminishing air pocket beneath it. As the night progressed, the hull settled lower in the water and became increasingly unstable.

Those clinging to the hull endured exposure to freezing water. Lightoller organized the men into two balanced lines along the hull to counteract rolling caused by the swell. Despite these efforts, exhaustion and hypothermia caused several men to slip into the water and die during the night.

By morning, approximately 28 survivors remained alive. They were transferred to other lifeboats before the final rescue. Survivors from Collapsible B were later taken aboard RMS Carpathia via other lifeboats. The overturned hull itself was later sighted adrift by recovery vessels in the days following the disaster.

Selected occupants:
– – Harold Bride, Wireless Operator
– Archibald Gracie IV
– Charles John Joughin, Chief Baker
– Jack Thayer

Collapsible Lifeboat C (Starboard)

Launch time: Approximately 2:00 a.m.

Officer(s) in charge: Chief Officer Henry Wilde; First Officer William Murdoch; Quartermaster George Rowe (placed in command)

Rated capacity: 47 persons

Collapsible Boat B, found adrift by the ship Mackay-Bennett during its mission to recover the bodies of those who died in the disaster.

Estimated number aboard at launch: Approximately 43

Collapsible Lifeboat C was the first of the collapsible lifeboats to be launched. By this point, most forward lifeboats had already departed, and the remaining crowd on deck had shifted aft as the bow settled lower in the water.

During loading, a group of stewards and third-class passengers attempted to rush the boat but were driven back after warning shots were fired. After repeated calls for women and children, the remaining spaces were filled by men. Among those who boarded was White Star Line chairman J. Bruce Ismay, whose survival later became a significant source of public controversy. As the boat descended, Titanic's growing list caused it to strike the hull, and occupants were forced to fend it off using hands and oars.

Collapsible Lifeboat C was recovered by RMS Carpathia, arriving at approximately 5:45 a.m.

Selected occupants:
– J. Bruce Ismay
– Frank Goldsmith and his mother Emily
– William E. Carter

Collapsible Lifeboat D (Port)

Launch time: Approximately 2:05 a.m.

Officer(s) in charge: Chief Officer Henry Wilde; Second Officer Charles Lightoller; Quartermaster Arthur Bright (placed in command)

Rated capacity: 47 persons

Estimated number aboard at launch: Approximately 20

Collapsible Lifeboat D was the last lifeboat launched from the ship; all other boats were washed off the deck as it sank. Crew members strictly enforced the "women and children first" policy resulting in it leaving significantly under capacity. Two young boys, later known as the "Titanic Orphans," were brought by a passenger who did not board and perished in the sinking. Another young child, previously separated from his family, was also placed in the lifeboat by crew members. Several male passengers later entered the boat by jumping from A Deck. Following the sinking, Collapsible D received additional survivors transferred from Collapsible Boat A, increasing the number of occupants substantially. Collapsible Lifeboat D reached RMS Carpathia at approximately 7:15 a.m.

Selected occupants:
– Michel Marcel Navratil and his brother Edmond
– Mauritz Håkan Björnström-Steffansson
– Irene Wallach Harris

Chart of Survivors

Passengers	Category	Number on board	Percentage by total on board	Number saved	Number lost	Percentage saved	Percentage lost	Percentage saved by total on board	Percentage lost by total on board
Children	First Class	6	0.3%	5	1	83%	17%	0.2%	< 0.1%
	Second Class	24	1.1%	24	0	100%	0%	1.1%	0%
	Third Class	79	3.6%	27	52	34%	66%	1.2%	2.4%
	Total	109	5%	56	53	51%	49%	2.5%	2.4%
Women	First Class	144	6.5%	140	4	97%	3%	6.3%	0.2%
	Second Class	93	4.2%	80	13	86%	14%	3.6%	0.6%
	Third Class	165	7.4%	78	89	46%	54%	3.4%	4.0%
	Crew	23	1.0%	20	3	87%	13%	0.9%	0.1%
	Total	425	19.1%	316	109	74%	26%	14.2%	4.9%
Men	First Class	175	7.9%	57	118	33%	67%	2.6%	5.3%
	Second Class	168	7.6%	14	154	8%	92%	0.6%	6.9%
	Third Class	462	20.8%	75	387	16%	84%	3.3%	17.4%
	Crew	885	39.8%	192	693	22%	78%	8.6%	31.2%
	Total	1,690	75.9%	338	1,352	20%	80%	15.2%	60.8%
Total	All	2,224	100%	710	1,514	32%	68%	31.9%	68.1%

Pregnant Women of Titanic

By mid-January 1913, life had asserted itself in the quietest, most defiant way possible. Nine children had been born to women who survived Titanic. At least two other pregnancies had ended with the ship itself, carried down with their mothers into the Atlantic.

In first class, youth and privilege offered no shield from loss. Madeleine Astor was just eighteen and five months pregnant when she boarded with her husband, John Jacob Astor. He did not survive. Their son was born four months later, living nearly eighty years—a life begun in the long shadow of catastrophe.

The same pattern repeated itself with Mary Graham Carmichael Marvin and Mary Eloise Hughes Smith, both eighteen, both newly married, both widowed before their honeymoons had ended. Each returned home alone and gave birth later that year to children who would grow up knowing their fathers only as names and absences.

Second class carried its own ledger of survival and erasure. Mary Emma Corey, already pregnant and returning from Burma, was lost entirely. Others lived. Argene Del Carlo, barely eight weeks along, survived while her husband did not; she gave birth months later in Italy, far from the life she had intended to build in America.

Juliette Laroche, traveling with her husband and two young daughters, was also early in pregnancy. She and the girls were saved. Her husband was not. Back in France, she gave birth to a son who would carry forward a family nearly erased in a single night. Ada Mary West survived with her daughters, four months pregnant, while her husband perished; her third child was born that September. Adal Na Allah, scarcely seventeen, survived the sinking only to lose both her husband and, shortly after birth, her infant son.

In third class, survival was rarer still. Maria Mathilda Backström, seven months pregnant, escaped aboard the last lifeboat successfully lowered. Her husband and brothers did not. She returned to Finland and gave birth that summer. Hannah O'Brien, four months pregnant and traveling from Ireland with her husband, survived alone. Her daughter was born in September and lived well into old age.

Together, these births formed a quiet countercurrent to the disaster's arithmetic of death. They did not erase the loss, but they complicated it—proof that even in the aftermath of catastrophe, the future arrived anyway, carried by women who had already endured more than history would ever properly record.

A Canine Eulogy

The ship's log says that twelve dogs boarded Titanic:

- Two Airedales
- King Charles Spaniel
- Fox Terrier
- Chow Chow
- Poodle
- French Bulldog
- Great Dane
- Newfoundland.
- Two Pomeranians
- Pekingese

One woman lived the rest of her life haunted by the memory of her Poodle clinging to her pajamas as she left her cabin and her dog behind.

Another passenger, Ann Elizabeth Isham, boarded the Titanic in Cherbourg with her Great Dane. She refused to leave the ship without her dog, which was too large to fit in a lifeboat. Ann Isham was one of four first-class female passengers who died on the Titanic. There are accounts, though unsubstantiated, that her body, with her arms wrapped around the dog, was later found by a recovery ship.

Margaret Bechstein Hays's Pomeranian (Lifeboat 7)

Margaret Hays, a first-class passenger, wrapped her Pomeranian in blankets and took it with her into Lifeboat 7, the first boat launched.

The three surviving dogs of Titanic

John Jacob Astor and his Airedale, Kitty, and Gamin de Pycombe with his champion French Bulldog.

The Harpers' Pekingese "Sun Yat Sen" (Lifeboat 3)

Henry and Myra Harper, also first-class passengers, took their Pekingese, "Sun Yat Sen," into Lifeboat 3. As to the rationale for how a pet made it into a boat while so many people did not, Henry S. Harper, a publishing magnate, replied: "There seemed to be lots of room, and nobody made any objection."

The Rothchilds' Pomeranian (Lifeboat 6)

First-class passenger Elizabeth Jane Rothschild hid the dog until the following morning, when the RMS Carpathia rescued those on Lifeboat 6. The crew had initially refused to take the dog on board, but Elizabeth insisted. Mr. Rothschild didn't survive the sinking.

Preview of *Ladies First, Titanic's Reckoning with Wealth & Worth*, By Alina Rush

Available at bookstores and online at Amazon.com, Barnes and Noble, and www.unboundpressbooks.com

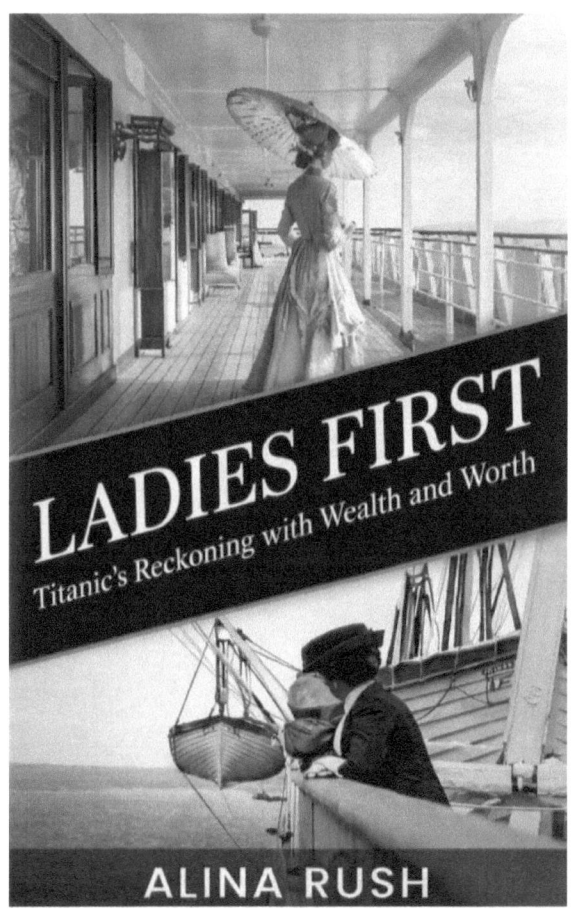

Introduction

Women and Children First

The phrase "Women and Children First" did not originate with the Titanic, but it was on that ship that the rule became a myth. In the decades since the disaster, it has been repeated as evidence of Edwardian chivalry—proof that, in extremes, society protected its most vulnerable. The reality was more complicated, more uneven, and more revealing.

On the night of April 14, 1912, the instruction to prioritize women and children was neither universal nor consistently enforced. It was filtered through class, geography, authority, and timing. Where a woman stood on the ship—physically and socially—often mattered as much as her gender. The rule did not operate in a vacuum. It operated on a vessel already divided by design.

Titanic was not one ship but several stacked vertically. First-class women were closest to the boat deck, spoke the language of the crew, and were accustomed to deference. Second and third-class women slept deep below, navigated unfamiliar corridors, and often traveled alone or with children in tow. Between them were the ship's working women—stewardesses—tasked with maintaining order, comfort, and calm, even as the situation deteriorated.

The rule women and children first was never written into maritime law. It was custom, not statute. Custom depends on who enforces it, who obeys it, and who is able to benefit from it. On Titanic, enforcement varied by officer. Obedience varied by passenger. Access varied by class.

For some women, the instruction functioned as intended. They were awakened early, guided to the deck, and placed into lifeboats with relative speed. For others, the rule arrived too late, or not at all. Some never heard it, and others physically could not reach the lifeboats. Some faced constraints because of language barriers, locked passageways, or the simple arithmetic of distance and time.

The survival statistics tell only part of the story. Women survived at higher rates than men overall, but that headline obscures sharp internal divisions. First-class women survived at extraordinary rates. Third-class women did not. Children's survival depended almost entirely on class and age, as we will see from the story of Rhoda Abbott. Gender alone did not save lives; proximity, privilege, and help did.

The phrase also obscures the cost borne by women whose labor made evacuation possible. Stewardesses guided passengers, translated instructions, distributed lifejackets, and maintained order in the corridors. Many delayed their own escape or never attempted it. Their adherence to duty—shaped by employment, gender expectations, and obedience—became another invisible factor in who lived and who did not.

Women and children first was not a promise. It was a principle unevenly applied on a divided ship. Understanding what it actually meant—who benefited from it, who enforced it, and who paid for it—reveals far more about the Titanic than the myth ever has.

This is not a story of chivalry fulfilled. It is a reckoning with how gender and class interacted under pressure, and how those interactions shaped the outcomes of one of the most scrutinized disasters in modern history.

Chapter 1 — A Ship of the Gilded Age

What we call the Gilded Age is but the glittering surface of a deeper struggle.

— Mark Twain

The Turkish Baths, April 14, 1912

THE TURKISH BATHS WERE tucked within the heart of the ship, below the promenade and away from the Atlantic wind, where heat could be sustained, and illusion perfected. The Edwardian fascination with the "Oriental" bath—heat, tile, ritual purification—had traveled from London clubs to Atlantic liners, and White Star understood that first-class women expected more than cabins and courses. They expected experience. The baths were part of that promise, and maintaining them required precision.

To step inside was to forget the ocean. Tile replaced timber, and vibrant mosaic floors gleamed under electric light. Geometric designs of an Eastern motif patterned the walls in turquoise and cream. Marble basins curved outward like open palms, and brass fixtures shone against the warmth. Neatly stacked white, thick towels waited to be unfurled by women of privilege.

Steam permeated the air. Not heavy or oppressive but controlled. Designed. A gentle hum from the ship's hidden machinery filled the room, muffled by tile and plaster. The baths were insulated from motion. Here, Titanic did not feel like steel and rivets. She felt like a hotel in Cairo or a private club in London. Heat, tile, and order: a sanctuary within steel.

Recreation of Turkish Bath, Titanic

First-class women entered wrapped in robes, speaking in low voices about Paris, about Fifth Avenue, and about the bracing air on deck. The bath softened them. Heat loosened conversation. Slippers slid against tile. Jewelry was removed and placed carefully aside. Gloves folded, and hair loosened from pins. The ritual was deliberate. Light reflected off the marble, and outside, the April air in the Atlantic Ocean remained sharp and cold.

A warm room first, to allow the body to adjust. Then hotter air, encouraging perspiration. Cooling rooms afterward, with chairs arranged for rest beneath electric sconces. Some women lingered to read. The Atlantic felt far away.

The baths were not merely a service, but a statement: to bathe at sea was to experience civilization on the water; that refinement need not yield to salt and wind. It meant the Atlantic could be crossed without surrendering comfort.

Admission required a first-class ticket, where class was softened but not erased. The attendants kept the system intact. Maude Slocombe was among them, checking the temperature of the steam chamber and ensuring the basins were properly filled and drained. She arranged combs and brushes where they would be easy to find. She refreshed the towels and ensured the baths were spotless. Maude understood that luxury is maintained through invisibility. The room must feel effortless, as if the towels were folding themselves. Maude's presence was part of the illusion: calm, competent, and discreet.

It is difficult to imagine a greater contrast: below decks, immigrant mothers wrapped infants against the draft; above, women reclined in warmth, insulated from the Atlantic's bite. And on the night of April 14, when the tremor moved through steel and tile alike, steam shivered almost imperceptibly before settling again. At first, it felt like nothing more than an interruption—a minor correction in motion.

The illusion held for a few minutes longer.

Heat lingered, towels remained folded, but outside breath was visible, the stars bright and indifferent. The boat deck was alive now with motion that did not resemble leisure, and the ocean was pressing against the hull below. Maude did what she had been hired to do, moving women toward safety. She spoke in a steady tone and trusted the structure above her. Luxury had been her department. Now survival was.

And the line between them was thinner than tile.

--------------------❖--------------------

Titanic's story began in the spring of 1909, on the gray edge of Belfast Lough, where men in flat caps and heavy boots walked beneath a wall of steel. Above them, the ribs of a new ship—Yard Number 401—rose higher than any building in the city. She was not yet called Titanic. She was an idea first: an answer to rival shipping lines, a promise of crossing the sea in unmatched comfort and safety. Their boots struck timber planks slick with rain.

At the turn of the century, the Atlantic had become a corridor of competition, as empires traded people and goods across the North Atlantic. Cunard boasted speed, while other lines promised glamour, famous passengers, and record-breaking passages.

The White Star Line responded with a different promise: not just the fastest crossing, but the most comfortable and prestigious way to reach America. From this promise came a trio of great liners, the Olympic-class ships—Olympic, Titanic, and a planned third sister, later named Britannic—intended to command the Atlantic in 1911, 1912, and 1913. They would not race the ocean; they would dominate it.

In Belfast, the shipyard reshaped itself to meet that ambition. Gantries climbed higher than church spires. On March 31, 1909, workers laid the keel, and from that line of steel, the skeleton climbed.

Riveters hammered red-hot bolts into place, sparks falling like brief, furious stars. Workers hoisted and fixed steel plates, and the hull thickened day by day against wind and tide. For more than two years, the work did not stop. Nearby sheds turned out fittings for cabins that would rival grand hotels on land. White Star's goal was clear: a ship large enough to carry wealthy travelers in luxury and, at the same time, to move thousands of emigrants in third-class and hundreds of crew members across the ocean in a steady, profitable stream. Speed mattered, but prestige mattered more.

Titanic was designed to carry about 2,435 passengers and around 900 crew, a small floating city divided by class and function, yet sharing the same steel hull and the same cold ocean. Her designers built in fifteen watertight bulkheads and doors that could be closed from the bridge, a system widely praised at the time and often cited as a reason she was described in newspapers and advertisements as practically "unsinkable."

The Launch

At 6 am on Tuesday, 2 April 1912, as people along the lough watched her slide into the water, a single firework exploded against a turquoise sky to announce the moment. Women in hats stood beside factory workers, and people lifted children onto their shoulders. The ship—still hollow and unfinished—moved down greased slipways and entered the gray sea to the sound of whistles and cheers.

She was named Titanic, and she was already famous, already a symbol of what modern steel and steam could achieve.

Titanic departing Belfast for sea trials on 2 April 1912. Public Domain.

Even unfinished, she was the largest moving object ever made by human hands. Inside her hull, for nearly a year more, carpenters, electricians, upholsterers, and decorators turned steel into rooms. Carpenters carved English oak into panels that replicated those in the Palace of Versailles. Staircases rose beneath glass domes. Carpets were chosen with debate and patience. Below, emigrants who had never seen electric light in their own homes would find cabins fitted with iron bunks and enamel washstands.

The ship was becoming layered, not only by deck but also by expectation.

Luxury and Distance

Ten decks rose above the Atlantic, each one narrowing the field of experience. From the outside, the ship appeared unified—a sweep of steel and funnels, a society under steam. Inside, it divided itself.

First Class

First class was theater. Passengers entered through wide gangways into corridors trimmed in polished wood and brass. Electric light—still a marvel to many travelers— glowed steadily from chandeliers and wall sconces.

Rooms were not uniform; they were themed. First-class suites featured walls with motifs inspired by Jacobean halls, as if European heritage could be contained within steel. English oak paneling was carved in relief; drawing rooms reflected Louis XVI style; French gilt and carved balustrades decorated the spaces; and the grand staircase rose beneath a glass dome. Versailles had been miniaturized and encased in steel. Designers recreated aristocratic interiors within the hull of a steamship, compressing centuries of taste into a single voyage. Here, history floated. Telephones, a marvel of their time, were even installed.

We think of Titanic in black and white, but in reality, it was saturated with color. Velvet. Polished wood. Gilt trim catching the electric light. Forest green carpets lay against ornate wallpaper designs in orange and red. The upholstery was rich, burnished gold. Carpet selection alone occupied the designers for two hours. The question of how many lifeboats were needed would be asked and answered in 15 minutes. After all, it was designed to reassure the wealthy, not to anticipate failure.

First Class Bedroom on Titanic

The famous grand staircase rose beneath a glass dome, its balustrades crafted with precision. There were four dining rooms, à la carte restaurants and a Parisian café. There were smoking rooms, sitting rooms, and writing rooms. There was the Turkish bath, a squash court, and a gymnasium with mechanical horses and rowing devices allowing for exercise at sea. The message was clear: civilization need not surrender to the ocean.

Second Class

Second class did not glitter, but it did not apologize either. The corridors were painted in light tones that softened sconces' electric glow. There was no carved oak or gilt, just polished wood trim and clean lines. Cabins were compact but private. Iron bedsteads fixed to the wall and crisp white bedding stretched tight. Hooks for coats. A narrow wardrobe. A mirror that did not flatter, but did not distort.

The Second-Class Dining Saloon lay on the Saloon Deck, broad and orderly, capable of seating hundreds at long, neatly arranged tables. White tablecloths under proper china, and silver polished to a quiet shine. No orchestra swelled here, no carved ceiling overhead—but the service was steady and correct. Meals arrived in courses. Soup steamed in porcelain bowls, and bread was passed hand-to-hand.

This room hosted a different kind of conversation. Not about estates and inheritances, but about positions secured or waiting. A clerkship beginning in Chicago. Letters received, wages expected, or a school term in Boston. A husband establishing himself in Seattle, or a new position in a Vermont household. Second class was full of people mid-trajectory.

There was a library where mahogany chairs stood beneath shelves of books. Writing desks faced windows where the Atlantic stretched in steel-blue calm. Women wrote letters by electric light—reassurances sent ahead, descriptions of the ship's steadiness, remarks about the chilly April air on deck. Men withdrew to the Smoking Room, its walls paneled in dark wood, its air thick with talk and tobacco.

Second-Class Dining on Titanic

On clear afternoons, passengers walked the open deck assigned to them, leaning into the wind that smelled of salt and coal smoke. The railings were polished brass, deck planks clean and pale beneath sensible shoes. Children darted between deckchairs. Mothers called them back.

Second class occupied a middle altitude on the ship— close enough to glimpse first-class elegance if one knew where to look, far enough above steerage to avoid its density. The staircases were narrower, but they were navigable and direct. Movement upward required less negotiation. This mattered, though no one yet knew it would.

For second-class passengers, the voyage felt modern, measured, and attainable. There was no spectacle here. They had not purchased extravagance. They had purchased passage with dignity. And for four days, the ship delivered exactly what had been promised.

Third Class

Below, assurance thinned. Third class would carry the future of the Atlantic migration: Irish girls bound for domestic service, Scandinavian laborers, Jewish mothers traveling alone with infants, and boys just tall enough to call themselves nearly men.

Advertisement for Third Class, Titanic

The accommodations were not squalor, but containment. Third-class cabins were small and stacked deep within the hull. They were enclosed, not open berths, arranged in compartments toward the lower decks where they felt the hum of electrical systems below. Bedding was provided, and meals were served in common dining rooms rather than requiring passengers to cook their own provisions. Privacy was limited, and families were grouped by gender and status according to regulation. Corridors were narrower, but for many immigrants, this was progress.

Earlier generations had crossed in open berths with little sanitation and less privacy. Titanic offered dignity. Families could close a door. The décor did not mimic Versailles, but utility. There was a small washbasin fitted with running water, an indulgence for many travelers who had known only shared pumps ashore.

Yet even here, color existed. Light came from electric fixtures, yes—but without chandeliers or gilt. Iron bunks with green-and-white bedding replaced carved bedsteads. The ship felt modern and hopeful. The modern age had reached even here.

The physical space between a third-class cabin and the boat deck was measured in stairways, turns, and time. This distance mattered. The difference between a first-class woman's promenade and a steerage mother's bunk was not merely aesthetic. It was logistical.

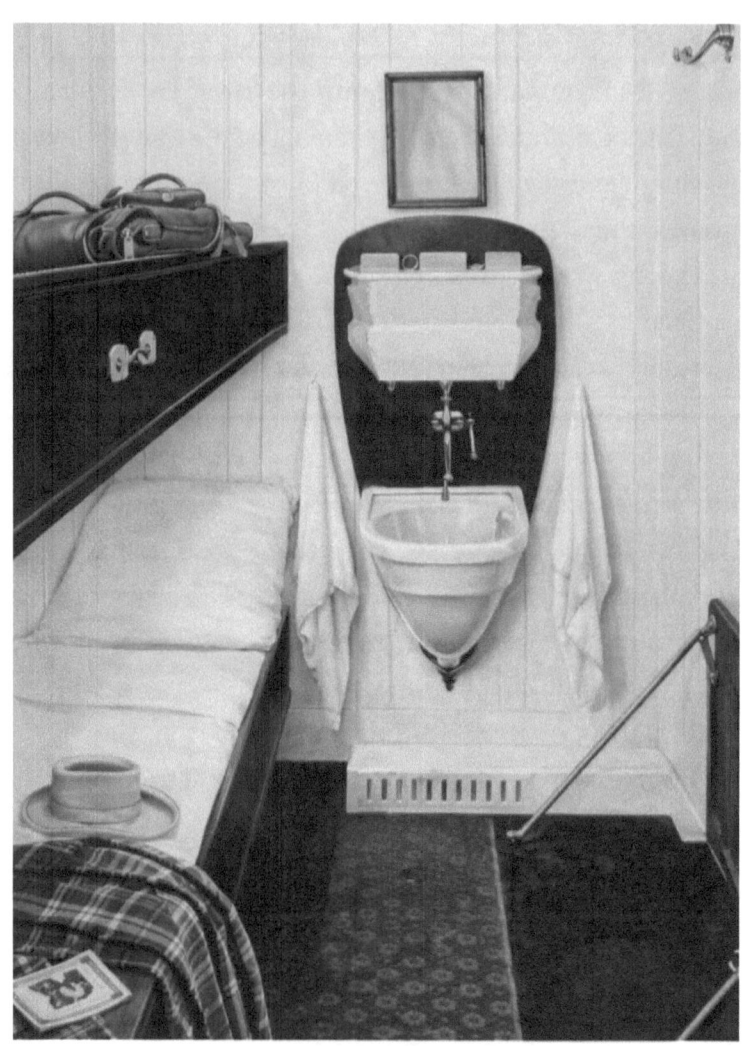

Third Class Accommodations

www.ingramcontent.com/pod-product-compliance
Lightning Source LLC
Chambersburg PA
CBHW020447130626
46549CB00001B/330